SHAKE-SPEARES

SONNETS.

Neuer before Imprinted.

———————————

———————————

AT LONDON
By *G. Eld* for *T. T.* and are
to be folde by *william Aspley.*
1609.

TO . THE . ONLIE . BEGETTER . OF.
THESE . INSVING . SONNETS.
M^r. W. H. ALL . HAPPINESSE.
AND . THAT . ETERNITIE.
PROMISED.

BY.

OVR . EVER-LIVING . POET.

WISHETH.

THE . WELL-WISHING.
ADVENTVRER . IN.
SETTING.
FORTH.

T. T.

THE DE VERE CODE

Proof of the true author of
SHAKE-SPEARES SONNETS

Jonathan Bond

www.realpress.co.uk

Acknowledgements:
Huge thanks to everyone who has given me the support and
encouragement to bring this book to fruition. It would not
have been possible without the insights and helpful criticism
of those who have kept me buoyant through draft,
redraft and re-redraft. Much love to:
Mum, Kath, Jo, Sam Parks, Siobhan Redmond,
Bobby Goodale, Sîan Williams, Lucy Bailey,
Bruce Fraser, Mark Rylance, Claire van Kampen,
Alan Macgregor, Mark Turner, Bill Leahy, Julia Cleave
and everyone I've had the privilege to
share Shake-speare with, on stage—or off.

Published by Real Press
www.realpress.co.uk
+44 (0)1273 35 80 80

Real Press is part of Real Group (UK) Ltd
Canterbury Innovation Centre
University Road
Canterbury
CT2 7FG

Registered in the UK, Company No. 6556128

Printed in the UK by MPG Biddles Ltd

British Library Cataloguing in Publication Data
A catalogue record for this publication is available from the
British Library
Library of Congress Cataloguing in Publication Data
A catalogue record has been requested

ISBN: 978-0-9564127-9-9

FOR MY DARLING CHRISTINE
AND THE INCOMPARABLE BRETHREN
HARRY AND STANLEY

CONTENTS

PROLOGUE

What sublimity of mind must have been his who conceived how to communicate his most secret thoughts to any other person, though very far distant, either in time or place . . . speaking to those who are not yet born, nor shall be this thousand or ten thousand years . . . and with no greater difficulty than the various arrangement of two dozen little signs upon paper? Let this be the seal of all the admirable inventions of man.

Galileo Galilei, Dialogue, 1632

I n the late summer of 1609, Galileo Galilei held a small lentil-shaped disc up to the light, and peered through the greenish glass. He could see one or two tiny blemishes and a couple of trapped bubbles of air towards the edges—not ideal—but bearable perhaps. The technique was nothing new, he used the same methods by which spectacle makers had been producing the "glass-lentil" or lens (as Latin would have it) to correct the long-sightedness of ageing scholars for three centuries past. But over months of trial and error in his Padua workshop, Galileo had pushed the limits of the technology further and further.

Ground and polished over a period of weeks, this was the largest and finest lens he had yet achieved. Placing it back in its wooden frame, he took up another, similarly-sized glass sliver, but whose sides—like two saucers back to back—curved inwards. An altogether more recent invention, this "concave" lens had been bringing the distant world into sharper relief for those, usually younger, sufferers of short-sightedness, for less than a hundred years. But not long after its invention, rumours began to circulate of other, stranger devices obtained by using the two lenses in combination. There were whispers of magical instruments for viewing one's enemies across vast distances, or for reading the writing on coins dropped in a field.

In 1608, almost out of the blue, these speculations coalesced into fact. Two merchants made patent applications to the Netherlands States General in The Hague for a new device, christened the "perspective glass". Incorporating the two types of lens at either end of a long tube, the perspective glass could be used for "seeing faraway things as though nearby". Deemed too easy to replicate, the devices—though highly commended—were refused a patent by the Dutch authorities. News of the designs spread rapidly, and across Europe, the race to develop the telescope was on.

Already a leading philosopher, mathematician and physicist at the University of Padua, the 45-year-old Galileo sprinted ahead of the field in developing the new instrument. While the competition struggled to achieve two or three times magnification, by August 1609 Galileo had more than doubled the power of their best efforts. As the winter drew on he perfected a telescope with lenses encased in a tube of lead, capable of a then astonishing twenty times magnification, pointed it towards the heavens, and began a series of astronomical observations.

For the first time, mankind, through Galileo's eyes, saw great mountains and deep craters on the surface of moon, saw that the Milky Way was born not of the breast of the goddess Hera but consisted of stars and more stars, and that beautiful, mysterious, hitherto undreamed of constellations existed deep in space. Then, on 7 January 1610, through the lenses of this most powerful of telescopes, the planet Jupiter hove into view. Galileo immediately noticed something new, and in his notebook jotted down that "three little stars, small but very bright, were near the planet". The pinpricks of light, two on the east side and one on the west on a horizontal plane, made him wonder: how could they seem as bright as the surrounding fixed stars yet be invisible to the naked eye?

The next evening, Galileo found Jupiter again and to his astonishment, saw that the three pin-pricks of light were now together—and on the opposite side of the planet. Two nights later the three became two, and on the fifth night another "star" was born from nowhere, making four. As the nights progressed, and the Jovian companions danced back and forth, always along the same horizontal path, Galileo noted their sizes and movements until the conclusion became inevitable: the dancing stars were satellites, in circular motion about Jupiter just as our own Moon circles the Earth.

Galileo quickly realised that what he had observed was the first experimental evidence that the centuries-old Ptolemaic cosmology, which placed the Earth at the centre of creation with all other celestial inhabitants revolving about it, could not be correct. More observations followed. He pointed the telescope towards the celestial goddess of love, Venus, and saw that she waxed and waned just as our own Moon does. Like her sister goddess, Cynthia, then, Venus was a satellite too — but orbiting *the sun*.

Galileo knew that his observations confirmed the radical theory, first advanced by Copernicus less than 100 years previously, that the Sun, not the Earth, was the central body of the known Universe. He also knew that he was playing with fire. The Ptolemaic theory underpinned all religious and political thinking in the Western world. To make public his findings would be to contradict the Pope. Heresy. Torture, retraction, then — if he was lucky — death. But nothing weighs so heavily as a secret. And this was a big one. Galileo had to *tell* someone. And so he first communicated his discoveries by letter to his trusted collaborator, the champion of the Copernican theory, resident in the relative safety of Germany: Johannes Kepler. And to protect them both, he used a Latin *code*:

HAEC IMMATURA A ME JAM FRUSTRA LEGUNTUR
O.Y.

which translates as:

"These unripe things are now read by me in vain"

but is also an anagram of:

CYNTHIAE FIGURS AEMULATOR MATER AMORUM

which means:

"The mother of love imitates the phases of Cynthia."

That Galileo and Kepler knew and used codes was by no means exceptional. The 16th century saw an explosion of secrecy, as politics became international politics and embassies began to spring up in the major cities across Europe. Official and unofficial communications became a natural target for interception, and methods of concealing and revealing their content became a matter of critical importance for both religious and secular powers.

In 1563, cryptography—the art of creating secret messages—assumed a central role in English politics. In that year, the occultist, mathematician and astrologer, Dr John Dee, obtained for Sir William Cecil—Queen Elizabeth's closest advisor—a manuscript copy of an unpublished work entitled *Steganographia*. Written in 1499 by a German monk, Johannes Trithemius, after a visitation from an angel in his dreams, it had not been easy to come by, said Dee, being a work "for which a thousand crowns have been by others offered, and yet could not be obtained". The reason was simple. *Steganographia* (literally "covered writing"), fabled as a book of magic and sorcery whose author possessed extraordinary powers, contained the most advanced methods of encypherment then known.

The book enabled Cecil (whom we shall come to know much better, later, as Lord Burghley) and the Queen's new spymaster general, Sir Francis Walsingham, to distribute and gather intelligence via a network of agents across Europe in their war against the Pope and the Spanish Empire. The techniques it contained would be used to crack codes revealing a Spanish plot to land insurgents on English shores in 1577, and, in 1586, it would have its most notorious triumph in foiling the Babbington Plot to overthrow Elizabeth and install the Catholic Mary Queen of Scots on the English throne. In a sting involving intercepted letters and a compromised cypher, Walsingham and his agents engineered a trap that led Mary to put her own head on the executioner's block.

In 1606, after a hundred years being copied and passed from hand to hand around Europe, Trithemius's masterwork was finally published. The perceived threat to the interests of the Church was so immediate and so great that in 1609, the Vatican placed *Steganographia* on its Index of Prohibited Books, rendering its possession heresy.

· · ·

As Galileo ground and polished his way towards a new understanding of the cosmos — and a life sentence at the hands of the Inquisition — and the Pope was labelling the mere possession of *Steganographia* punishable by death, a London publisher, oblivious to the moons of Jupiter, presented a small sheaf of love poems to the public gaze. Containing 154 short and one long poem, the immediate impact of this literary event was less than revolutionary. But over the following centuries the author would come to be known as perhaps the greatest pioneer of humanity's inner world, and the work itself would stand as one of the greatest puzzles in the history of literature. The volume was entitled *SHAKE-SPEARES SONNETS*.

Such is the power of the words contained within, that generations of readers have pored over each and every one, hoping to better understand the myriad layers of meaning of these poems, to uncover their *secrets*. And secrets there certainly are, though they are the secrets of love rather than war. The idea that love sometimes must be concealed is not new, of course. In 1BC, when Ovid wrote "A letter is also safe and escapes the eye when written in new milk; touch it with coal dust and you will read," he was advising clandestine romantics in *The Art of Love*.

On the one hand, the poems seem to present the most intimate portrait of a man, his loves, his trials and dispositions, and the characters to whom, and about whom he is writing. The first 17 poems, the "procreation" sonnets, are addressed to a beautiful young man — the Fair Youth — whom the author urges to beget children as the only surety against death:

> *And nothing gainst Time's scythe can make defence*
> *Save breed to brave him, when he takes thee hence.*
> *Sonnet 12*

The vast majority of the poems, sonnets 18–126, are also a addressed to a young man—perhaps even the same one—to whom the poet writes some of the most famous words of love in the English language, commencing with perhaps the simplest and most celebrated of all:

Shall I compare thee to a summer's day?
Sonnet 18

The remainder of the sonnets cover a range of disparate themes; they mark the appearance of the notorious "Dark Lady", the mistress for whose affections the author competes with a rival (perhaps again the Fair Youth) and also hint at some deep disgrace for which the poet pays with desolate self-loathing.

And so the puzzles begin. Coming from the hand of any other great writer, such revelations would be meticulously bolted to the cast-iron framework of the author's biography. And yet generations of readers have found the Shakespeare of the title page the most elusive character of all those to whom *SHAKE-SPEARES SONNETS* refers. As leading scholar Professor Jonathan Bate put it in *The Genius of Shakespeare*, right at the point one thinks he might reveal himself, Shakespeare is able to "perform the very disappearing act which is always available to a dramatist who loses himself in his characters, but which should by rights be impossible for a lyric poet who writes in the first person." Was Shakespeare even writing about himself at all, some have wondered, or rather penning exercises in style from the perspective of artistic detachment?

Adding to the sense of mystery are the 30 words that precede the poems: a curiously aloof, awkwardly phrased dedication, ostensibly written by the publisher, to an unknown dedicatee. These words have remained a puzzle for editors, who by turns have struggled to explain the meaning of this prefatory address in a way that is consistent with the circumstances of its publication.

TO.THE.ONLIE.BEGETTER.OF.
THESE.INSVING.SONNETS.
Mr.W.H. ALL.HAPPINESSE.
AND.THAT.ETERNITIE.
PROMISED.
BY.

OVR.EVER-LIVING.POET.
WISHETH.

THE.WELL-WISHING.
ADVENTVRER. IN
SETTING.
FORTH.

T.T.

From faint contemporary rumblings in the Elizabethan and Jacobean literary milieu, the theory began to be voiced in the 17th century that perhaps Shakespeare *himself* was a cypher. Perhaps the plays and poems published under the name of "William Shakespeare" were not actually written by the man to whom they are usually ascribed—an actor from Stratford-on-Avon in the county of Warwickshire who became a shareholder at the Globe theatre on the south bank of the river Thames in London. Strangely, in the 19th and 20th centuries, as literary detective work unearthed new evidence from the period, these voices grew more rather than less insistent. The view among these "anti-Stratfordians" as they came to be known, is that the plays and poems attributed to William Shakespeare could not have been written by a man who left no books behind him, who had no interest in seeing his daughters learn to write, who mentioned not a single work of his own or any other in his will, in whose hand there is not one surviving letter—nor any addressed to him by those prolific letter-writing poets of his time, and whose death went unremarked by those same contemporaries who would apparently extol him seven years after his demise with the publication of the *First Folio* of Shakespeare's plays.

Thus the idea was born that there might be (at least) *two* Shakespeares. On the one hand there is *Will Shaksper* (as he shall be known herein), the Globe actor and shareholder who it is assumed was also a land- and property-owning burgher in his home town of Stratford-on-Avon. On the other hand there is *Shake-speare*—as I shall call him—a playwright and poet who published under a pseudonym, and whose plays were performed at the Globe, presumably with the explicit foreknowledge of the Stratford man.

My own interest in the *Authorship Debate*, as it has come to be known, was first sparked when I read the late John Michell's book *Who Wrote Shakespeare?* while working in the acting company at the reconstructed Globe theatre in London in 1998. Taking no sides, Michell elaborated the arguments for a number of the alternative candidates proffered as most likely to have written the works of the Bard. I was intrigued in particular by Michell's suggestion that a simple cypher in the dedication indicated that the Elizabethan nobleman Edward de Vere, 17th Earl of Oxford, was the likely author of the sonnets.

I began to follow the trail of evidence through the websites and books devoted to establishing the claims of the various candidates. All the accounts I came across relating de Vere to the sonnets had something in common: each presented *part* of the evidence, but no source presented *all* of it. Whether because individual authors were only concerned to deliver their own discovery, or whether they were simply not aware of the other research, there did not exist a single detailed, clear exposition of all the salient points. I decided, therefore, to write one.

Then something surprising happened. I noticed fortuitously a piece of evidence that had not previously been commented upon. Although it was an extension of an already published argument, it was still quite a surprise, not least because it seemed so obvious that I couldn't believe it had been missed. I investigated and indeed no-one had pointed it out before. More importantly, the discovery significantly strengthened the argument for de Vere and so I thought it would be of great interest to anyone intrigued by the Authorship Debate.

However, the fact that something so important had not been spotted provoked me to look at the evidence again, in case anything else had been overlooked. Thus it was that on a warm evening in early June 2009, almost exactly 400 years since the day that *SHAKE-SPEARES SONNETS* first appeared in print, I saw something that made the hairs on the back of my neck stand on end.

There in front of me was an entirely new cypher. Like the moons of Jupiter, it had been there all along, unregarded, but in that instant of recognition, I was transformed from being an Authorship agnostic to an out-and-out heretic. Further investigation of what had been revealed led to yet another entirely new piece of evidence and to discovery after discovery relating to the context of the composition and publication of the poems. Suddenly, what had before seemed like a strong set of arguments that de Vere wrote the sonnets, now had all the hallmarks of *proof*—not only that he had written them, but of who they were written about, and to whom they were dedicated.

Hence, *The De Vere Code*. In Part One, the context into which the sonnets were published is outlined, and the questions those circumstances raise about who was publishing them, and why. In Part Two, the proofs concerning de Vere's authorship and the subject and dedicatee of the poems are presented in detail. In Part Three, an explanation of the genesis of poems is given that for the first time addresses all the conundrums surrounding their composition and publication, and places the work as a whole in its historical context as one of the most significant cypher-texts ever written.

The poet Ben Jonson was notoriously short on deference to the talent of his contemporaries, but when he said of Shake-speare, "I loved the man, and do honour his memory, on this side idolatry, as much as any," he set the benchmark for our modern appreciation of the works of the Bard. Whatever one's intellectual perspective, an idol of sorts is what Shake-speare has become. Insofar as that perspective incorporates the basic elements of humanism—compassion, reason, justice, truth, love—then the plays and poems of Shake-speare stand pre-eminent as the texts through which those humanist urges reflect, assess, and reinvent themselves.

The image of Shake-speare as the humble Stratford glover's son, strolling into the cultural big bang that was Elizabethan London and channelling the very elements of being through his pen into the human heart by sheer transcendent talent, is appealing. Indeed, it is the *terra firma* about which the universe of orthodox authorship beliefs revolve. Thankfully, although that orthodoxy is tremendously hostile to those who offer evidence that this image is an illusion, no-one has yet ended up on the rack for their pains. And nor, I hope, will I.

I. RIDDLES

On 20 May 1609, a disgruntled Thomas Thorpe hurried up Ludgate hill. Ahead, the rotting carcass of St Paul's, with its once-towering spire reduced to a lightning-splintered stump, and its dazzling stained glass perforated by the missiles of Reformation rioters, only added to the general mood of decay that gnawed at London's besieged inhabitants. Since Easter, Thorpe had been awaiting word from his printer, George Elde, that his latest commission was ready for delivery. Finally, that morning he had been able to collect a first proof copy from Elde's printshop at the sign of the White Horse in Fleet Lane, a slim "quarto" pamphlet of 80 pages containing 155 poems.

This was no time to be hanging around out of doors. London was in the grip of one of the most savage attacks of virulent plague that had been descending on the capital with increasing regularity for more than twenty years. In the spring of 1609 "the pest", as it was known, was killing up to a hundred a week in the city and causing anyone to flee who did not have either a very pressing reason to stay, or anywhere else to go. For three years, the theatres had been closed almost without respite. There was an urgency to complete business and be away as soon as possible.

Almost at the gates of St Paul's, Thorpe turned sharp left up Ave Maria Alley, reversing the route followed in the past by cowled monks as they wound their way down the crowded defile of Paternoster Row, reciting the Our Father on their way to the Corpus Christi mass. Now, the area around St Paul's was largely the domain of publishers, printers, binders and booksellers, jostling for space with prostitutes, gossip-mongers and hangers-on among the converted charnel houses and chantries of the cathedral churchyard.

There you could buy copies of the latest plays and poems by Ben Jonson or Thomas Dekker, pamphlets excoriating the Pope, King Philip of Spain and the French nation in general, and exhortations to support the colonial adventure in the New World. There were ballads and broadsides, the modern tabloid press in miniature, filled with true crime tales and fables garnered on exotic expeditions to the far-flung corners of the globe.

Two literary realities existed, however. At the rarefied level of the Court, the writing of poetry was primarily viewed as a pastime, a diversion from more serious concerns. True, it could reach great heights, and was taken very seriously by those who modelled their thought and their writing on the templates of the great masters of classical antiquity. Nonetheless, though any aristocrat worth his (or indeed her) salt might consider it a necessary part of their repertoire to be able to dash off a Petrarchan sonnet, the thought would have horrified them that they might *make money* out of it.

The professional writer was a new breed of animal still making its first tentative steps out from the shadows of the mediaeval religious and political social order. The emerging merchant class was importing, exporting and manufacturing as never before, and it needed writers to account both for the profits and the processes of wealth creation. And alongside this practical necessity, the floodgates opened for a tidal onrush of creative writing.

Remarkably, in this period, and for the first time in history, the intellectual elite and the newly literate working class began to encounter one another on something approaching an equal footing. The rendezvous for this unlikely meeting of minds was the Elizabethan playhouse. From the arrival of the first purpose-built public venue, The Theatre, raised in Shoreditch in 1576, it was in the playhouses of this era that Art met the artisan, the Court mingled with the commoner and writers of both classes became aware that despite differences in their circumstances, many of their artistic values were shared.

Most, if not all, of the writers for the stage at this time were also poets, and also wrote in some professional capacity for one or another of the aristocracy, or offices related to the Court. Conversely, while never officially condescending to write for the public stage, those members of the elite who had an interest in poetic writing often supported the artisans, both as their financial backers and employers and by acting as patrons to the theatrical companies of the day.

There was money to be made from creative writing, too, though more by those who published and printed than those who scratched out the words with quill and ink. Professional scribes were held in low esteem and fought tooth and nail to secure their reputation and hence their livelihood against attack. And attacks were frequent: from other writers, slandering and libelling one another, and more than occasionally resorting to physical violence to underline their point; from the religious authorities, ever observant against the degradations into which the libidinous fraternity of authors was certainly leading every congregation; and from the Crown, whose determination was to use all means at its disposal to ensure that nothing was said that contradicted the Divine Right or threatened the established order.

Suppression was ruthless. In 1599, an edict from the Archbishop of Canterbury and Bishop of London ordered the seizure and burning of *all* the works of the writers Hall, Marston, Marlowe, Davies, Nash and Harvey. Of Nash and Harvey, the order added "that none of their books be ever printed hereafter". The order also outlawed the publishing of satires and epigrams full stop. Hundreds of works were destroyed in similar purges.

But, as Thomas Thorpe passed under the portico of Abergavenny House, it was the issue of copyright that was at the forefront of his mind. Newly acquired as the headquarters of the Worshipful Company of Stationers, Abergavenny House was a suitably grand testament to the growing status of this city guild. Established by Royal charter in 1557 with a remit from Queen Mary to stamp out the publication of Protestant propaganda, the Stationers' Company now controlled both the means of publication, and the censorship of content. No printer could put paper between his presses unless licensed to do so by the

Master and Wardens of the Stationers' Company. No publisher could lawfully print a word unless similarly authorised.

Enforcement was placed in the hands of the Stationers' Court of Assistants, which had powers to search properties and seize pirated or unauthorised publications, and to whip unruly apprentices, as well as fining or imprisoning their masters. When a Royal edict called for the suppression of some seditious satire or immoral ballad, it was the Court of Assistants of the Stationers' Company that confiscated the copies and put them to the torch.

As well as enforcing State censorship, the Stationers' Company also provided the best, indeed the only, means for a publisher to ensure that his livelihood was protected. By presenting a copy of a work to the Stationers' Company and entering its title in the Stationers' Register, the publisher (though not the author) was guaranteed exclusive rights to publish it.

Thorpe handed the freshly printed copy to the clerk, who passed it on to the Under Warden, who peered at it through his spectacles before delivering it to the Master Warden's office. A short while later, the clerk returned and duly filled out an entry in the Register:

> *Entred for his copie vnder thandes of master Wilson and master Lowndes Warden a Booke called SHAKESPEARES sonnettes.*

A tedious but necessary job done, Thorpe hurried back to Elde's shop to instruct the despatch of copies of the now-legitimised publication to two booksellers: William Aspley, whose shop was then at the sign of The Parrot in St Paul's churchyard, and William Wright, whose shop was at Christ's Church Gate near Newgate. How many copies Elde delivered to each is not known.

And the rest, as someone once said, is silence.

Reception

Of the birth in print of what would come to be the most celebrated poems in the English language, not another word was said. The *SONNETS* (as I shall hereafter refer to Thorpe's edition) disappeared into the Jacobean literary melting pot with nary a ripple to mark its passing. And where the paper trail ends, the mystery begins.

On the face of it, it seems the book was either hardly read or not liked, or both. The next direct reference to the *SONNETS* in print comes with an entirely new and much-altered edition of the poems in 1640, a full 31 years after the original publication. No-one, it seems, was motivated to produce another edition of this extensive collection either during the Stratford man's lifetime, or at his death in 1616, or even in conjunction with the publication of Shake-speare's theatrical works, the *First Folio* of 1623. Remarkably, in the period up to 1640, from the three poet-titans, Ben Jonson, John Donne and John Milton, it seems not one word was said in print on the subject of the *SONNETS*. The silence is all the more remarkable given that two of Shake-speare's other poems were certainly in demand in 1609.

Back in 1593, Shake-speare had exploded into the literary first rank with the publication of an epic poem retelling the story of the doomed affair between the goddess Venus and her mortal love Adonis. With its courtly dedication to the 20-year-old Henry Wriothesley, 3rd Earl of Southampton, and elevated-yet-knowing language, *Venus and Adonis* scored a direct hit among all classes of literate Elizabethans. The follow-up, 1594's *Lucrece*, while slightly less popular, was still a huge success, and together the two poems sold and sold, going through at least 26 editions in the years up to 1655. Given that level of popularity, one might imagine a queue round the block in anticipation of the publication of not one, but 155 new poems by a poet already held in high esteem by his contemporaries.

There are grounds for ramping up the anticipation even further. In 1598, the clergyman and critic Francis Meres published a tome

7

entitled *Palladis Tamia: Wit's Treasury*, "A Comparative Discourse of our English Poets, with the Greek, Latin, and Italian Poets", in which he rhapsodised thus:

> As the soule of Euphorbus was thought
> to live in Pythagoras : so the sweet wittie
> soule of Ovid lives in mellifluous &
> honytongued Shakespeare, witnes his
> Venus and Adonis, his Lucrece, his sugred
> Sonnets among his private frinds, &c.

Elsewhere in this famous early review of Shake-speare, Meres also provides the first critical mention of a number of his plays, thereby providing the only contemporary reference to Shake-speare as a playwright *and* sonneteer. What is clear is that 11 years before the sonnets were published, some people, a select group perhaps— Shake-speare's "private frinds"—had seen some of the poems, and others knew they existed. And this makes it seem all the stranger that when the *SONNETS* was published in 1609 there was no ripple of interest—not even from Meres, who one imagines would have been delighted to get his hands on, and perhaps review, the first edition.

The mystery only deepens when the literary context of the *SONNETS* is taken into account. The archetypal 14-line sonnet form was the invention of the 14th-century Italian humanist Petrarch, and the architect of the English sonnet cycle was Sir Philip Sidney, whose seminal sonnet sequence *Astrophel and Stella* was published posthumously in 1591, and spawned many imitators. And yet, as Katherine Duncan-Jones points out, the *SONNETS* is "in important respects both anti-Petrarchan and anti-Sidneian." Crucially, and uniquely for any sonnet sequence of the period on this scale, it is mostly addressed to a very real young man, not an idealised female such as Petrarch's "Laura", and Sidney's "Stella". This alone made the poems radical. So, given that the *SONNETS* is clearly on a par with *Astrophel and Stella* in terms of ambition, and Shake-speare's reputation as a poet, it seems remarkable that the contemporary audience was not breathless with excitement that Shake-speare's "response" to Sidney was to be published. And when those poems hit the streets, it is baffling that there was no mad rush to read, anatomise and further respond to this reinvention of the form; a reinvention seen today as so complete that the poems exist in a category all of their own: the Shake-spearean Sonnet.

Today, 13 known copies remain of Thorpe's edition. Paradoxically, this is taken to confirm the relative disinterest with which the *SONNETS* was received in 1609. Pamphlets, printed on the cheap brown paper of the time, were not built to last. A popular work, the theory goes, passed from hand to hand among an audience hungry for the latest thrills, would quickly be read to destruction. Of many of the numerous editions of *Venus and Adonis*, for example, only single copies have made it to the present day intact. So it is thought that the 13 relatively well-preserved copies of the *SONNETS* betoken a certain covetousness—intentional or otherwise—regarding Thorpe's publication. Either the copies lay untouched on a shelf or in a drawer, rarely brought out for examination, or perhaps they were hidden from the authorities, or were kept out of circulation, in the way a limited edition might be jealously guarded today.

How quickly that initial print run dwindled to the 13 surviving copies is another unknown. But for the remainder of the 17th, and much of the 18th century, access to the sonnets would be almost exclusively via the second, 1640 edition. Published by John Benson, it was a very different beast indeed from its predecessor. That Thorpe's edition of the poems would not be republished intact for over a hundred years in itself suggests that his book remained the province of a small, and ever-decreasing, circle of admirers. This apparent "failure" of Thorpe's edition has never been satisfactorily explained. However, consideration of Benson's edition can shed some light on the puzzle.

Reincarnation

In November 1640, London was in turmoil. King James had been dead for fifteen years, and his son Charles was at odds with Parliament, at war with the Scottish Bishops and fast running out of capital with which to maintain his increasingly fragile grip on the country. It was a good time to be in business for the likes of John Benson, however, as he made the trip from his overflowing shop in Chancery Lane to the Stationers' Office at Abergavenny House. A canny operator, Benson had made a success of himself mostly at the downmarket end of the publishing trade. In addition to more highbrow fare, he was equally at home producing cheap popular ballads and the broadsides that were disseminating gossip and increasingly destabilising the authorised routes of political and religious discussion.

But regardless of the direction in which John Benson's moral compass pointed, his business sense seems to have been sound. In 1640, he was also in the process of acquiring a second shop, in St Dunstan's Churchyard on Fleet Street. Five years earlier, Thomas Thorpe had retired from publishing, and London, to see out his days in the 15th-century almshouses at Ewelme in Oxfordshire. The exact date of his death is unknown, but in the absence of family relations continuing in the profession, Thorpe's copyrights would certainly have been up for grabs. Even if he had not died in the run-up to 1640, a sharp-eyed publisher such as Benson might well have taken advantage of Thorpe's departure from London, and preemptively "acquired" the soon-to-lapse rights to the *SONNETS* for himself.

Benson clearly saw a gap in the market. The *First Folio* of Shakespeare's plays of 1623 had been followed by another edition in 1632, and the poems *Venus and Adonis* and *Lucrece* were still regularly reprinted. Since 1609 however, no new edition of Shake-speare's sonnets had been published. With a copy of Thorpe's edition, and a bit of artistic license, Benson set about filling that gap.

The resulting quarto edition, *POEMS:WRITTEN BY WIL.*

SHAKESSPEARE. Gent., has subsequently been lambasted as fraudulent, misguided, piratical, and homophobic. Shake-speare scholars have queued up to hurl insults at it. Stanley Wells, editor of the Oxford Shakespeare series and chair of the Shakespeare Birthplace Trust, was comparatively kind when he called Benson "underhand". Less so, were John Kerrigan, editor of the Penguin *Sonnets*, who cited the "unforgivable injuries" done by Benson, and Arden *Sonnets* editor Katherine Duncan-Jones, who summarised Benson's intentions as "outrageously piratical and misleading".

In his edition, Benson reprinted all but eight of the 154 sonnets and included the long poem *A Lover's Complaint*, as Thorpe had. He added some songs from Shake-speare's plays, and other poems which had previously been published in an unauthorised collection entitled *The Passionate Pilgrim*. What has raised the ire of subsequent editors are his other "improvements". Benson rearranged the order of the sonnets from that given by Thorpe, grouping them into categories and adding his own "banal" (Wells again) titles. If that wasn't bad enough, in order—so the story goes—to ameliorate the sonnets' homoerotic content, he changed pronouns from "he" to "she", and even omitted some poems altogether. To rub in some salt, he added a number of verses by other authors without acknowledging them, and in his preface palmed the whole lot off as Shake-speare's own.

Benson's aim appears quite straightforward. It was to produce a best-selling companion volume to the *First Folio* of Shake-speare's plays, first published in 1623. He wanted his edition to appeal to the broadest market and to be readily identified as having the same authority as the former work. His method was simple, he made the *POEMS* (as I shall refer to it) look like the *First Folio*.

Now in its second edition, the *First Folio* gathered together 36 plays, 18 of which had never before been printed. The edition commenced with a dedication by Ben Jonson, "To the Reader", facing the title page on which was presented a portrait of "Shake-

speare" by the young engraver Martin Droeshout. There followed
a dedicatory epistle, "To the most noble and incomparable paire of
brethren, William and Philip Herbert, the Earls of Pembroke and
Montgomery". Then came a preface by the publishers, followed by
a long eulogy, "To the memory of my beloved the AUTHOR", again
by Jonson. Three more short poems followed—and then the plays.

For *POEMS*, Benson followed suit, including a portrait,
dedication, introductory preface, and dedicatory poems. Notably,
Benson's dedication deliberately mimics Jonson's in the *Folio*. The
two texts are as follows. First Jonson's:

This Figure, that thou here seest put,
It was for gentle Shakespeare cut;
Wherein the Grauer had a ftrife
with Nature, to out-doo the life :
O, could he but have drawne his wit
As well in brasse, as he hath hit
His face; the Print would then surpasse
All, that was ever writ in brasse.
But, since he cannot, Reader, looke
Not on his Picture, but his Booke.

Then Benson's:

This Shadowe is renowned Shakespear's! Soule of th'age
The applause! delight! the wonder of the Stage.
Nature her selfe, was proud of his designes
And joy'd to wear the dressing of his lines
The learned will Confess, his works are such,
As neither man, nor Muse, can prayse to much
For ever live thy fame, the world to tell,
Thy like, no age shall ever paralell.

Benson's first phrase, "This *Shadowe* is renowned Shakespear's!" directs the reader to the engraved portrait, as does Jonson's opening, "This *Figure*, that thou here seest put, It was for gentle Shakespeare cut". The theme of "nature" is borrowed from Jonson, too. Benson's phrase "Soule of th'age, The applause! delight! the wonder of the Stage" is lifted wholesale from Jonson's eulogy, *To the memory of my beloved, the Author*:

> *I, therefore will begin. Soule of the Age!*
> *The applause! delight! the wonder of our Stage!*

In addition to imitating the *First Folio*, Benson's introductory preface referenced Thorpe's *SONNETS* dedication too. First the *SONNETS* dedication:

TO.THE.ONLIE.BEGETTER.OF.

THESE.INSVING.SONNETS.

Mr.W.H. ALL.HAPPINESSE.

AND.THAT.ETERNITIE.

PROMISED.

BY.

OVR.EVER-LIVING.POET.

WISHETH.

THE.WELL-WISHING.

ADVENTVRER. IN

SETTING.

FORTH.

T.T.

The words highlighted are all echoed by the text I have capitalised in Benson's preface:

> To the Reader.
>
> I here presume, under favour, to present to
> your view some excellent and sweetly composed
> poems of Master William Shakespeare, which in
> themselves appear of the same purity the author
> himself, then living, avouched! They had not the
> fortune, by reason of their infancy in his death, to
> have the due accommodation of proportionable
> glory with the rest of his EVER-LIVING works
> ... certain I am my opinion will be seconded by
> the sufficiency of THESE ENSUING LINES.
> I have been somewhat solicitous to bring this
> FORTH to the perfect view of all men, and in so
> doing glad to he serviceable for the continuance of
> glory to the deserved author in these his poems.

It is clear that as well as revealing his debt to Thorpe, Benson was making a conscious effort to make *POEMS* the companion to the *First Folio* by aping its style, and lifting phrases directly. But Benson also says something slightly peculiar in the above preface, something that is very revealing about his psyche as he prepared the *POEMS* for printing in 1640. In the second sentence of the preface, he says of the verses and their author, "They had not the fortune, by reason of their infancy in his death, to have the due accommodation of proportionable glory with the rest of his ever-living works...". Benson seems to be suggesting that the poems have never been seen before, and that the reason for this is that they were only written shortly before the author's demise. This is fascinating, because it reveals that at the time he was preparing the *POEMS* for publication,

14

Benson felt his customers would need a convincing explanation of why Shake-speare's poems had suddenly turned up, years after his death, if they were to be persuaded that the poems were genuine.

Of course, Benson knew the poems had been published before, by Thorpe. Yet, it is clear he was confident that the audience for the *POEMS* would accept his explanation; that they would be satisfied that the reason for the sudden, and very late, appearance of the "complete" Shake-speare poems (excluding the copyrighted *Venus and Adonis* and *Lucrece* of course) was that the author had died without managing to get them published.

Crucially, this implies Benson believed that few, if any, of the potential purchasers would have been aware of Thorpe's edition. Indeed, the fact that Benson aimed to get away with a straight falsehood implies that he thought almost no-one knew the *SONNETS* existed. And this suggests that, by 1640, the *SONNETS* had all but disappeared from view. However he had come by his copy (which might even have simply been missing the sonnets he did not include), Benson clearly thought he had something that very few, if any, of his contemporaries were aware of.

Wily operator that he was, the entrepreneurial Benson judged his market well. The *POEMS* was popular enough that far from disappearing, it formed the basis for every reprinting of the sonnets for the next 126 years. It can be concluded then, that there was nothing inherent in the content of poems that prevented them from being marketable. And this seems to leave two alternatives with regard to Thorpe and his first edition: either he was a naive and incompetent pirate who produced an edition so badly judged that no-one was interested in buying it; or he knew exactly what he was doing, but the motivation behind the publication he oversaw was more complex than the straightforward pursuit of profit.

Taking the former possibility first, was Thorpe inept? A brief consideration of his career up to 1609 would suggest not.

Who was Thomas Thorpe?

When the sonnets landed in the lap of Barnet-born Thorpe, he had been publishing in his own right for eight years. An innkeeper's son, he began his apprenticeship under the stationer Richard Watkins in 1584, and became a freeman of the Stationers' Company ten years later. By 1609 he was an established publisher, if a somewhat unusual one. Unlike most of his contemporaries in the trade, Thorpe never owned a printing house or bookselling shop. In this respect he was one of the first of a new breed of independent publishers, overseeing a manuscript through printing and arranging for its distribution by a bookseller, a division of labour that would ultimately become the norm.

Thorpe's first solo venture was a Latin translation by the late Christopher Marlowe entitled *Lucan's First Book*, which he published in 1600. He was given the copyright by Edward Blount, a highly regarded publisher, who in 1623 would go on to co-publish the *First Folio*.

The common practice among publishers at that time, especially up-and-coming ones, was to dedicate their productions either to those who had sponsored the work, or to some eminent person whose patronage was sought for the future. Instead, Thorpe acknowledged Blount's act of generosity by dedicating *Lucan's First Book* to him. The dedication is entertaining, if lengthy, but it is worth sampling to appreciate how different it is to the dedication Thorpe later printed in the *SONNETS*:

TO HIS KIND AND TRUE FRIEND, EDWARD BLUNT

Blunt, I propose to be blunt with you, and, out of my dulness, to encounter you with a Dedication in memory of that pure elemental wit, Chr. Marlowe, whose ghost or genius is to be seen walk the Churchyard, in, at the least, three or four sheets. Methinks you should presently look wild now, and grow humorously frantic upon the taste of it. Well, lest you should, let me tell you, this spirit was sometime a familiar of your own, Lucan's First Book translated; which, in regard of your old right in it, I have raised in the circle of your patronage ... One special virtue in our patrons of these days I have promised myself you shall fit excellently, which is, to give nothing; yes, thy love I will challenge as my peculiar object, both in this, and, I hope, many more succeeding offices. Farewell: I affect not the world should measure my thoughts to thee by a scale of this nature: leave to think good of me when I fall from thee.

Thine in all rights of perfect friendship,

Thomas Thorpe

The generous tone and humorous spirit of the dedication are most evident. Thorpe clearly enjoys wordplay, his style is clear and his points are straightforwardly made. Above all, Thorpe's tone is confident, he is clearly at home in his medium and in the world of words.

Regardless of his lack of a printing press or shop premises, Thorpe continued in steady business over the next five years, and by 1605 it seems his reputation for reliability and quality was growing. For in that year Thorpe was brought into contact with perhaps the most demanding, certainly one of the most controversial, and—in his own opinion at least—the greatest dramatist of the age: Ben Jonson.

Jonson's career was taking off in 1605. He was becoming a fixture in Court circles both as a composer of verse and as the most sought-after writer of masques, the lavish entertainments loved by King James and his wife Anne. He was also a magnet for controversy.

Back in 1597, while a member of the Admiral's Men, the acting company in residence at the Rose Theatre nestled behind the Clink prison on the south bank of the Thames, Jonson appeared in a "lewd" and "slanderous" play by Thomas Nash entitled, *The Isle of Dogs*. Though it has been lost to posterity, it is thought that the play may have gone so far as to satirise the Queen. Certainly the Isle of Dogs itself, across the water from Greenwich, was a ripe metaphor: at that time it was both the location of one of the Royal palaces and also a notorious sewage-infested swamp. Elizabeth, apparently, was not amused, and three of its actors, Gabriel Spenser, Robert Shaw, and Jonson were thrown in the Marshalsea prison, while its author fled to Great Yarmouth. For two months Jonson languished in prison, a 25-year-old aspiring writer unable to avail himself of the influential patrons who would bail him out of later run-ins with the authorities. By October 1597 the Privy Council was satisfied no serious wrongdoing would be uncovered, and the three actors were released.

Perhaps galvanised by the experience, within the year Jonson had written his first theatrical hit, the latinate comedy, *Every Man in His Humour*. He was also back in prison. On 22 September 1598, in a duel at Hogsden Fields (now Hoxton) Jonson fought and killed Spenser, the actor with whom he had shared a cell the previous summer. Pleading guilty, Jonson escaped hanging only thanks to his classical education. Able to recite Bible verses in Latin, the statute of "Benefit of Clergy" commuted Jonson's death sentence to the forfeit of his property, a period of incarceration in Newgate, and a branding. The latter he received on his thumb, "T" for "Tyburn"—the notorious venue of public execution.

Following his release, Jonson remained in combative mood. For the next few years, in what became known as the "War of the Theatres", he traded insults with a number of his fellow playwrights, including John Marston and Thomas Dekker. The combat was waged both via coded references in their plays and in extremis, physically, with Jonson later claiming to have beaten Marston and disarmed him of his pistol. In one of his most barbed satirical swipes, thought to originate from around this time, Jonson attacked another of his contemporaries in a famous epigram. Entitled, *On Poet-Ape*, the tone is set in its scathing first four lines:

> Poor POET-APE, that would be thought our chief,
> Whose works are e'en the frippery of wit,
> From brokage is become so bold a thief,
> As we, the robb'd, leave rage, and pity it.

The Poet-ape, according to Jonson, was either a writer or actor, or both, whose own efforts were but "frippery" (rags), but who believed himself to be the principal play-maker of the day. After initially buying up old plays, Poet-ape had become so confident that he began to steal wholesale from others and pass all off as his own work. It has long been a staple of the anti-Stratfordian case that the subject of Jonson's jibe might have been Shaksper. It is suggested by Authorship agnostics too, that the poem is one of several contemporary instances of the accusation that Shaksper was not the author of the works being presented under the "Shake-speare" name at the Globe.

Though by 1605 the "Poetomachia", as the War of the Theatres was christened by Dekker, was apparently over, Jonson's reputation for arrogant self-promotion, superiority and intolerance—largely self-created—never left him. In a later year he made a pilgrimage on foot to his ancestral home of Scotland, and spent time at the home of the poet William Drummond of Hawthornden. According to Drummond's report of the meeting, Jonson left a lasting impression:

> He is a great lover and praiser of himself; a contemner
> and scorner of others; given rather to lose a friend than
> a jest; jealous of every word and action of those about him,
> (especiallie after drink, which is one of the elements in
> which he liveth;) ... Oppressed with fantasie, which hath
> ever mastered his reason, a generall disease in many poets.

Jonson did not suffer fools gladly, nor was he easy to get along with, but in 1605 he had a project in hand which was bound up with his public reputation as a writer, and for which close collaboration was essential. Interestingly, it was Thomas Thorpe who undertook the task.

Thorpe and *Sejanus*

In 1603, Jonson's play *Sejanus: His Fall* was first performed by the King's Men at the Globe theatre. It was not well-received. In the words of contemporary poet, William Fennor:

> With more than human art it was bedewed,
> Yet to the multitude it nothing shewed.
> They screwed their scurvy jaw and look't awry,
> Like hissing snakes adjudging it to die.

As Jonson himself later pointed out, "[it] suffered no less violence from our people here than [its hero] did from the rage of the people of Rome". If a critical mauling wasn't enough, the play landed him in trouble with authority once again. According to his own testimony, he was called before the Privy Council on a charge of "popery and treason" relating to the play. Jonson laid the blame for these accusations firmly at the door of the Duke of Northumberland. The Duke, Jonson complained, harboured a grudge against him for beating one of his servants.

The play had been a failure on the stage, but in his inimitable way, rather than moving on, Jonson decided to set the record straight. He re-wrote *Sejanus* in 1604, prefacing it with an epistle making it clear that this play:

> ...is not the same with that which was acted on the public stage; wherein a second: pen had good share: in place of which, I have rather chosen to put weaker, and no doubt, less pleasing, of mine own, than to defraud so happy a genius of his right by my loathed usurpation.

Jonson's decision to remove all traces of the "second pen" is intriguing, of course. But given Drummond's assessment of Jonson's character, one could easily be forgiven for thinking that he is being less than chivalrous in his assessment of the merits of his collaborator's contribution. But whether or not Jonson was blaming its reception on his co-author's failings, he was clearly on a mission to clear the play's name and establish it as the exemplary work he had no doubt it really was.

To this end, Jonson planned to publish *Sejanus* with a degree of literary authority previously unheard of for a work from the public playhouses. In addition to re-writing the play, he provided extensive marginalia, a practice more usually reserved for scholarly and religious texts. These notes provide explanations and source references for *Sejanus*, underscoring at every turn the author's learning. In a fabulous display of paranoid authorial pedantry, Jonson determined to annotate his critics into submission.

Given the reputation of the man, one could well imagine many a publisher flinging down the shutters and taking an extended vacation when Jonson in such a mood came to call. The complexity of the layout of the text Jonson had in mind would make it a labour-intensive job, and hence expensive. What would the financial return be likely to amount to on a play that had been both critically panned and a political irritant?

Indeed, the first person to whom Jonson offered *Sejanus* did, it seems, pass on the opportunity of publishing it—perhaps once he realised what Jonson was expecting. *Sejanus* was entered into the Stationers' Register in 1604 by none other than Edward Blount, but rather than undertaking to publish it himself, in 1605 he transferred the copyright to his friend and one-time protégé, Thomas Thorpe.

To Thorpe, Jonson represented the opportunity of a major step up the professional ladder. On the contemporary scene, Jonson's star was burning brightly and so it would make sense for Thorpe, still a relatively small player, to grab Blount's "gift" with both hands. When one remembers Thorpe's gently mocking dedication to Blount's first act of generosity, taking on Jonson seems to fit too with Thorpe's sense of humour and audacity. Importantly, Thorpe was confident in himself, and called on the services of his friend and preferred printer, George Elde to work with Jonson to produce the edition.

The team, it seems, worked well together. Modern editors have remarked on the quality of presentation of the *Sejanus* text. As Jonson scholar Jonas Barish commented: "The exactness of the marginal annotations, the closeness with which the typography conveyed Jonson's metrical intentions, and the corrections made in proof all suggest that Jonson oversaw the printing himself." This is what one would expect given his interest in the end result.

But as anyone who has ever spent time working in an editorial office knows, a difficult writer can quickly make a complex task exponentially fraught. In such a situation the person standing between the printer and the author performs a vital role in oiling the wheels of the process, acting as an intermediary proofreader, interpreting instructions and massaging sensitive egos.

Thorpe, it seems, was exemplary in this role. *Sejanus* was published in 1605, with dedication, preface, and commendatory verses from several of Jonson's "well born or scholarly friends" to see it on its way. Jonson was impressed enough with Thorpe to collaborate with him on his published output for the next three years, including his courtly masque *Hymenai* in 1606, the great *Volpone* in 1607, and in 1608 two more masques. Though none of these was so demanding in its presentation, for three years at least, Thorpe was the publisher in whom Jonson placed his trust. After 1608, it seems the relationship ended.

Whatever caused the later rift with Jonson, by 1609 Thorpe had become a publisher with a profile. In addition to his numerous other clients, he had established a close working relationship with perhaps the best-known professional poet of the day — with connections at the highest level at Court, even to King James himself—and had proved himself capable of working for this most demanding of clients. And now, in Thorpe's grasp was a manuscript of poems from the hand of Shake-speare, the author of the best-selling *Venus and Adonis* and *Lucrece*, the only writer to whom Jonson would have the slightest qualms about declaring himself the superior.

However he obtained it, Thorpe would have understood the sales potential of the manuscript he was about to publish. And yet, instead of applying his wit, ingenuity, and professional contacts to produce and promote a lavish work, bedecked with commendatory poems, perhaps sponsored by an earl or two to give it an extra special lift off, Thorpe produced a damp squib, shorn of commendation, bereft of ornament. The title, *SHAKE-SPEARES SONNETS*, was odd in including the author's name in the possessive as if this was the sum total of his output, with no more sonnets likely to appear. No other living author had done this before. The only other collection so titled was the seminal sonnet sequence published in 1591 as *Syr. P.S. his Astrophel and Stella* in memory of its author, the *late* Sir Philip Sidney (again prompting the suspicion that the *SONNETS* was somehow responding to its predecessor). At the same time, the quality of presentation, though basic, was good—as one would expect from Thorpe and his printer Elde.

All in all, it seems implausible to suggest that Thorpe either did not know what he was doing, or that he did not care. And this makes it clear that whatever the explanation is for the "failure" of the *SONNETS* to thrive, some other motivation for publication than simply making money must have been at play.

Thus it is that the 30-word dedication prefacing the *SONNETS* comes to loom so large in this story. With no answers to be found in the contemporary record, no comments from those who might have read it, the contradictory nature of the edition itself and such a gaping hole in the cultural *milieu* where one would expect these poems to subsist, it is of course the very peculiarity of the dedication that excites and stimulates those seeking an answer to the mysteries surrounding this publication. And as we shall see, when it comes to the dedication itself, though the puzzles are simple, their implications are profound.

The Enigmatic Epigram

TO.THE.ONLIE.BEGETTER.OF.
THESE.INSVING.SONNETS.
Mr.W.H. ALL.HAPPINESSE.
AND.THAT.ETERNITIE.
PROMISED.

BY.

OVR.EVER-LIVING.POET.
WISHETH.

THE.WELL-WISHING.
ADVENTVRER. IN
SETTING.
FORTH.

When compared with Thorpe's dedication to Blount (page 16), the *SONNETS* dedication could not be more different in style, tone and presentation. Where the former is long, the latter is short. Where the first is facile and expansively humourous, the latter is blunt (sic), even awkwardly worded. The former delights in punning and witty colour, the latter is almost anti-poetic in its prosaic obstinacy. The former is immaculately laid out in a manner clearly designed to demonstrate Thorpe's technical competence, the latter, while its language defies poetic interpretation, is laid out on the page as if it *is* some sort of poem: its stanzas of odd length, its lines determined by no obvious grammatical or poetic rationale, and full-stops after every word.

That there is a single explanation that makes sense of all these unusual characteristics will soon become clear. To begin with, however, the two most obvious puzzles of the *SONNETS* dedication are, firstly, who is "Mr WH", and secondly, what is the meaning behind the phrase "that eternitie promised by our ever-living poet"?

The identity of Mr WH, and the sense in which he was the "onlie begetter" of the poems has intrigued readers of the *SONNETS* since at least the 18th century, prompting subsequent generations of scholars to identify at least eight different candidates. The alternatives broadly fit into three categories. "Mr WH" it is supposed, refers to either:

1. Shake-speare.
2. The person who procured the manuscript for Thorpe.
3. The person who inspired the sonnets.

Is Mr WH Shake-speare?

There is one small, but obvious problem with the theory that Mr WH is Shake-speare. The initials are wrong. To the eminent rationalist philosopher Bertrand Russell, however, this problem was not insurmountable. In the late 1950s, Russell suggested that the mystery of Mr WH might be the result of a typographical error, that a setter in the printshop of George Elde might simply have set an "H" where he should have inserted an "S" or indeed omitted an "S" before an "H". Thus "Mr WS" or "Mr W SH" became "Mr WH". This argument was adapted in *The Genius of Shakespeare* by Jonathan Bate as the most likely explanation. Bate expands Russell's point by observing that "one of the elaborate Elizabethan secretary-hand forms of capital 'S' closely resembles another secretary form of capital 'H'."

Even if this resemblance is true (and Bate does not give examples), the principal objection to this theory is on the grounds of plausibility. The idea of a misprint of this kind in the preface of such a noteworthy edition seems surprising. As anyone who has worked on an editorial desk knows, "typos"—as such mistakes are called—can creep into a publication at the most unexpected moments. However, authors rarely miss mistakes made by typesetters in their own work.

In the case of the *SONNETS* dedication, Bate and Russell fail to observe this crucial point. If, as they suggest, Thorpe wrote the dedication, then he must have been both author *and* final proofreader. Given what we know about Thorpe, his printer Elde, and their collaboration with Jonson, it strains credulity to imagine that Thorpe would have allowed such an obvious and major mistake *in his own words* to go through the presses. Unless he cared very little about the work in progress, he would certainly have carefully proofread the one part of the publication he wrote himself.

Is Mr WH the procurer?

The second broad group of theories is based on the premise that the phrase "onlie begetter" refers to the person who delivered the manuscript of the poems into Thorpe's hands. The question of how the sonnets came into Thorpe's possession is of course crucial. One candidate is the stepfather of Henry Wriothesley (the dedicatee of *Venus and Adonis* and *Lucrece)*, Sir William Harvey. For reasons that will be explained below, Wriothesley is also a prime candidate as the Fair Youth of the sonnets. Perhaps, the theory goes, his stepfather was having a clearout, and passed the manuscript on to Thorpe.

The problems with this theory are obvious. Given the sensitive nature of the subject matter of many of the sonnets—one man's profound love for another—it is to be wondered what Harvey would gain by making them public, except potentially the humiliation of his powerful stepson. There is no evidence that he had such a motive. Furthermore, Harvey was a knight who had married into a very influential family. Thorpe on the other hand was a commoner, a tradesman with no known connection to Harvey or his stepson. In the early 17th century, it was unlikely that Thorpe would address such a personage as "Mr WH".

The other main candidate as the procurer of the manuscript is a publishing associate of Thorpe's called William Hall. This theory, first advanced by Sir Sidney Lee in the 1890s, has the advantage that Hall does seem to have been a procurer of manuscripts and was known to both Thorpe and Elde. The "humble" nature of the dedication and appellation "Mr WH" sit more easily here. But why, then, does Thorpe not state Hall's name in full? For many years, the dominant theory was that Thorpe pirated the manuscript and the sonnets were published without the author's consent. Thus, while Hall might have obtained the manuscript, he might not wish to be easily identified, and so, it is suggested, might have asked Thorpe to use only his initials, providing some measure of protection.

The unauthorised publication theory has fewer adherents today, and scholars as eminent as both Jonathan Bate and Katherine Duncan-Jones agree that the evidence of Thorpe's professionalism suggests that the publication was authorised. But even if it was not, Thorpe himself had much more to lose in terms of reputation if an accusation of piracy was made, than the relatively unknown Hall, yet Thorpe's name was there for all to see on the title page. Hall is an inoffensive candidate, perhaps because of his relative obscurity. However, there will soon be very good reason to doubt him, too.

Is Mr WH the inspirer?

The third theory, and the one that has stimulated the most intense speculation, is, of course, that Mr WH is the person to whom, or about whom, the sonnets were written. The "onlie begetter", on this view, is taken to mean the inspirer, in the sense that his image has planted a seed in the poet's fertile imagination, and the sonnets are the fruit of this consummation. There is one rather important caveat to this theory.

Everyone is agreed that the sonnets are not all addressed to the same person. In that sense, there is no "onlie begetter" of the poems.

As was previously mentioned, the first 17 poems seem to be directed at a young man, urging him to marry and have children. Sonnets 18–126 are also mainly addressed to a young man, with whom the poet seems deeply in love, christened the "Fair Youth". Then follows a sequence to, and about, the poet's mistress, the "Dark Lady". The final two poems, and a good number scattered throughout the rest, are not addressed to a specific subject, but deal with general themes such as love, honour, shame, pride and so on.

It is thus assumed that "onlie begetter" is an allusion to Mr WH as the principal inspiration for the poems, and that both the suitor of sonnets 1–17, and the Fair Youth of sonnets 18–126 are the same person. An additional possibility, reading "begetter" literally as "getter" or "recipient" is that while only some of the poems were *inspired* by Mr WH, he nevertheless *received* all of them as a gift from the author. This latter theory is particularly appealing when one comes to consider the two noblemen most widely regarded as convincing candidates as the "onlie begetter": Henry Wriothesley, 3rd Earl of Southampton and William Herbert, 3rd Earl of Pembroke.

Henry Wriothesley

The 3rd Earl of Southampton, Henry Wriothesley, has already been encountered as the dedicatee of Shake-speare's landmark poems, *Venus and Adonis* and *Lucrece* in the early 1590s. As a candidate for the onlie begetter, he fits well too. Born in 1573, and by the turn of the 1590s stunningly handsome and highly favoured in Elizabeth's close circle, he was one of England's most eligible bachelors. Brought up as a Royal Ward in the house of William Cecil, Lord Burghley, the Queen's most trusted advisor and mentor, Wriothesley was educated at Cambridge, studied law at Gray's Inn, and was a devotee of the arts. From his 17th birthday in 1590 until his maturity in 1595, he was also under pressure from his guardian to marry. And not just anyone. Ever seeking to expand his dynastic influence, Burghley had in mind his own granddaughter Elizabeth as the perfect match.

Wriothesley prevaricated, delayed and deferred until in 1595, upon inheriting his full title, and no longer under obligation to anyone's will but his own—he refused to marry. So incensed was Burghley that he imposed a crippling fine on the young Earl. It was of course in this period, that Shake-speare published *Venus and Adonis* and *Lucrece* with their expansive—and in the case of *Lucrece* almost erotically charged—dedications to Wriothesley.

It is suggested that someone—perhaps Burghley—enlisted Shake-speare to encourage Wriothesley, and the relationship thus forged blossomed further, resulting in an ongoing "correspondence" of sonnets over a number of years. In addition, although, as Jonathan Bate says, "[i]nternal evidence needs to be treated with great caution", he goes on to elaborate possible wordplay linking the name of Wriothesley, which may well have been pronounced "Rose-ley" at that time, to the 14 instances of rose imagery in the sonnets. They commence with the second line of the very first poem:

> From fairest creatures we desire increase,
> That thereby beauties *Rose* might never die...
> *Sonnet 1*

The italics are Shake-speare's—the only instance in this poem. Adding to this references that suggest the mother of the Fair Youth is alive and his father dead at the time of writing, which fits Wriothesley in the early 1590s, Bate concludes, "the case for Southampton as the original patron/youth looks irrefutable."

However, the case for Wriothesley as the onlie begetter has two flaws. First, the initials in the dedication are the wrong way round. Again, this requires either the appeal to an unsatisfactory "typo" argument along the lines already refuted above, or a deliberate concealment of Wriothesley's identity by Thorpe—though concealing him as "Mr WH" seems less than ingenious. Both of these explanations give little credit to Thorpe's obvious intelligence.

The second, and more weighty objection is an extension of the argument against Wriothesley's stepfather, William Harvey, as the dedicatee. In 1609, when Thorpe is supposed to have been writing the dedication, Wriothesley was one of the foremost earls of the realm. If it would have been rude for Thorpe to refer to Wriothesley's stepfather as "Mr WH", the impertinence would have been unpardonable in reference to the 3rd Earl of Southampton. In addition, by alluding to Wriothesley in his dedication, Thorpe would be implicating the earl as the subject of the homosexual passion of the author, with more than a little hint that the feelings were mutual.

In this regard, it is worth bearing in mind that the Jacobean social order resembled one of the more violent and politically restrictive dictatorships of modern times. In this feudal society, power was exercised ruthlessly, and violence was the order of the day in suppressing dissent and enforcing the law. Stocking, whipping, beating, mutilation, branding, torture, hanging, drawing, quartering, burning, starving, disembowelling and beheading were only the better-known of the legitimate instruments of authoritarian control. In a society where the daily display of decaying body parts on the gatehouses of the capital served as a reminder of who was in charge, and massacre was always available as a last resort, respect for rank and title was a given. Shakespeare, too, was fully aware of the potential repercussions. As Duke Vincentio observes in *Measure for Measure*, "slandering a prince" deserved no less than "pressing to death, whipping *and* hanging."

Would a man in Thorpe's position have taken such a risk? Surely only if he was convinced he would not face retribution. For that to be the case, he would have to have been instructed by Shake-speare, or by Wriothesley, that "Mr WH" would not get him into trouble.

William Herbert

In many respects, the argument for the second prime candidate as Mr WH is a re-run of that for Wriothesley with a new set of dates, plus the attractive bonus that this time the initials match. In 1597, Lord Burghley was once again in the match-making business, and had again set his sights on a 17-year-old with prospects, this time William Herbert, as the ideal match for another of his granddaughters, Bridget. Again, the theory goes that in order to entice the eligible earl-to-be into the match, Shake-speare was employed, again either by Burghley, or perhaps Herbert's mother, the Countess of Pembroke (herself a patron of poets), to write verses encouraging William to cast his mind towards matrimony.

Although he would not inherit his full title of Earl of Pembroke until his father's death in 1601, in 1597 Herbert was already well known at Court. Seven years the junior of Wriothesley, he was a patron of the arts and a poet himself, and would keep a close circle of the most noted talents of the day, including John Donne. Ben Jonson, too, was one of Herbert's coterie, later remarking that "every New Year's Day he had twenty pounds sent him from the Earl of Pembroke to buy books".

Once again, the prospective son-in-law played hard to get, despite Burghley offering him a massive £3,000 dowry, and an annuity to commence on Burghley's (then imminent) death. Obstinately demanding the immediate commencement of the annuity, Herbert refused to commit, and ultimately pulled out of the deal. Burghley's granddaughter may well have got off lightly, however. During the latter period of their "engagement", Herbert was actually prosecuting an affair with one of the Queen's maids of honour.

Although to date no direct evidence has been presented of a connection between Herbert, Shake-speare and the sonnets around 1597, the circumstantial case is strong enough for Katherine Duncan-Jones to see Herbert's candidacy as Mr WH as "overwhelmingly attractive". Firstly, when the *First Folio* of Shake-speare's plays was later published in 1623, it was solely dedicated to William Herbert, by then Earl of Pembroke, along with his younger brother Philip, Earl of Montgomery—the so-called "incomparable brethren". It is likely that the poetry- and theatre-loving Herbert would have been an admirer of Shake-speare in the late 1590s when his plays were at the height of popularity.

Secondly, it will be recalled that in 1598 Francis Meres made his famous reference to Shake-speare's "sugard sonnets among his private frinds" in his treatise on contemporary poetry, *Palladis Tamia.* Perhaps, suggests Duncan-Jones, Shake-speare gave the poems as a gift to Herbert, who then circulated them among *his* close circle with the result that they became more widely known.

Thirdly, perhaps as a consequence of this wider audience, in 1599 two of the sonnets were published without the author's consent in an edition of 20 poems attributed to Shake-speare, entitled *The Passionate Pilgrim.* The edition, published by William Jaggard, was certainly unauthorised and contained many poems definitely not by Shake-speare under his name.

In 1600, the year after *The Passionate Pilgrim* appeared, Duncan-Jones draws attention to an often ignored entry in the Stationers' Register for:

A book called Amours by I.D., with certain other sonnetes by W.S.

Perhaps, she suggests, this could be what was known as a "staying entry", designed to prevent further unauthorised publication of the Shake-speare poems, following Jaggard's appropriation.

Taken together, the fragments of evidence create a picture of a flurry of sonnet-related activity just around the time of Herbert's marriage negotiations. The Herbert case sufficiently impresses Katherine Duncan-Jones to conclusively identify the Earl of Pembroke with the fair youth, and to suggest that the majority of the Fair Youth and "mistress" poems might have been written for him in the late 1590s. The early "procreation" sonnets could, she adds, equally have been written for Herbert or have been recycled by Shake-speare, having been originally inspired by Wriothesley.

Once more, the looming objection to this identification of "Mr WH" is that in 1609 it would have been unforgivably impertinent for Thorpe to address William Herbert, by then Earl of Pembroke, as "Mr". Enticingly, in the late 1590s, Herbert was still in his minority and might have been conceivably accounted "Master William Herbert". But, as with Wriothesley, in 1609, when Thorpe is supposed to have written the dedication, that appellation would have been extremely risky.

It should be added here that Thorpe himself was only too aware of the appropriate terms and formalities required, particularly in seeking patronage from Herbert. In 1610, the year after Thorpe published the *SONNETS*, he prefaced an edition of the lately deceased John Healey's translation of St Augustine's *City of God*, with a dedication to Herbert. The similarity with his earlier dedication of *Lucan's First Book* to Edward Blount is unmistakable, and leaves in no doubt the chasm Thorpe was spanning in deigning to address the earl at all:

> To the honorablest patron of the Muses and good mindes, Lord William, Earle of Pembroke, Knight of the Honorable Order (of the Garter), &c... Wherefore, his [Healey's] legacie, laide at your Honour's feete, is rather here delivered to your Honour's humbly thrise-kissed hands by his poore delegate. Your Lordship's true devoted,
>
> Th. Th.

Certainly a step up the ladder of obeisance from "Mr WH".

Who is the "ever-living poet"?

The second intrigue surrounding the dedication concerns the phrase "that eternitie promised by our ever-living poet". Who, it is wondered, is the "ever-living poet", and what is the "eternitie" they are promising? The instinctive assumption, prompted in no small measure by the prominence given to the phrase in the layout of the dedication, is that the "ever-living poet" is the author, Shake-speare and the eternity promised is that of seeing one's line continue through one's children, as repeatedly asserted in the first 17 sonnets. But, and it is a big but, in the early 17th century, the phrase "ever-living"—and on this point the authorities agree—is used only in reference to the dead. Shake-speare himself used it in this way in *Henry VI, part 1* when describing Henry V as "[t]hat ever-living man of memory". Shaksper, the Stratford player, was of course alive in 1609, and unusually, we know exactly what he was doing: chasing the Stratford trader John Addenbrooke for an unpaid debt of £6 (plus damages) through the local court in his home town.

There are three approaches to dealing with this anomalous phrase. The first is to ignore it. This is the route is taken by Duncan-Jones in the latest Arden edition of the sonnets. In her otherwise exhaustive dissection of the significances of the dedication, she expends not one drop of ink on this question, beyond the basic assumption that "our ever-living poet" refers to Shake-speare. A second route is taken by Jonathan Bate. As we have already noted, Bate believes that Mr WH is Shake-speare, and he takes this to imply that "ever-living poet" must refer to someone else—some already dead poet, perhaps Sir Philip Sidney, Edmund Spenser, or even Ovid. This is consistent, but one wonders (though Bate does not seem to) why a writer as competent as Thorpe did not simply name the anonymous author. A third suggestion is that "our ever-living poet" refers to God. Thus, the "eternitie" promised is everlasting life, and *that* is something only God himself—the creator, or Supreme Poet—can bestow.

None of the above explanations is completely satisfying, particularly since all three fail to do justice to the intuition that the "eternitie" promised in the dedication should mean *offspring*; that the promise of future life being made in the dedication is the same as that being made in the poems. The author of the dedication does seem to be referring specifically to the poet's insistence on children being the only sure guarantee of immortality. This is of course the best tie-in with both Herbert and Wriothesley, as the recipient/inspirer of the poems, if the whole enterprise was designed to encourage them to marry. But it also seems to require that the "ever-living poet" is the *author* of the sonnets—Shake-speare—and that seems to require him to be dead.

Jonson and the dedication

As Thomas Thorpe passed away in an almshouse in Ewelme, no doubt he had long since forgotten the slight pamphlet of poems that had occupied his time for a little part of the spring of 1609. He surely could have had no inkling of the controversy that would attend a collection of sonnets that seemingly sank without trace, never to resurface in his lifetime. Subsequently, the puzzling nature of the *SONNETS* dedication has intrigued readers and editors of the poems since at least the 18th century. But the first allusion to the *dedication*, as opposed to the poems, may actually date to the period immediately after the publication of the first edition. It comes from the pen of Ben Jonson.

Leaping forward seven years for a moment, in 1616, Jonson's star was at its zenith in the Court of King James, and in an unprecedented move for a living author, he published a collection of his plays and poems, entitled *Workes*. The poems, 133 of them, were included under the subtitle *Epigrammes*. They had originally been entered into the Stationers' Register in 1612, but were not immediately published, partly on account of Jonson's engagement as a tutor by Sir Walter Raleigh to accompany his unruly son on a tour of the Continent.

Each play in the collection was prefaced with the dedication that had accompanied its original solo publication, and the *Epigrammes* too bore a dedication, which it is possible to suppose was drafted as early as 1612. The dedication is expansive, and Jonson's opening salvo is striking:

MY LORD,

While you cannot change your Merit, I dare
not change your Title: It was that made it, and
not I. Under which Name, I here offer to your
Lordship the ripest of my Studies, my Epigrams;
which, though they carry danger in the sound,
do not therefore seek your shelter: For, when I
made them, I had nothing in my Conscience, to
expressing of which I did need a Cypher . . .

The implication is clear, says Duncan-Jones: "Jonson's stress on his adoption of a correct and unalterable 'title' — 'my Lord' . . . certainly sounds like a side-swipe at some other writer who has had the temerity to change it; and his assertion that the ensuing poems, though epigrams, a genre often regarded as dangerously personal or satirical, are in fact not so, may also allude to some other, more compromising or 'dangerous' form of poetry, which had indeed required the use of 'a cypher'."

Was Jonson alluding to Thorpe's *SONNETS* dedication, and by extension Shake-speare? The noble target of Jonson's devoted vassalage adds to the suspicion:

To the great Example of Honour, and
Vertue, the most Noble William, Earl
of Pembroke, Lord Chamberlain, &c.

Mr WH, of course.

Jonson's words are striking not only in their tone of rebuke — Jonson was well-known for adopting that attitude to his contemporaries. Extraordinarily, they draw direct attention to the possibility of the deliberate concealment of identity. Furthermore, whether it is the identity of Mr WH, or the author of the poems, or both that was being concealed, the issue Jonson sees as being at stake is clear from the remainder of his dedication. It is to do with making public matters which might be shameful or embarrassing either in the motives of the poet, or the revelations of the private life of their subject.

Jonson's relationship of patronage with Herbert was already well underway by 1609, and given his clear intention to publish the *Epigrammes* in 1612, it seems plausible that this dedication also dates from that year, and possibly earlier. This would place it in intriguing proximity to the *SONNETS*. Harking back, it will be remembered that Jonson's working relationship with Thorpe began in 1605, and continued until 1608, after which there is no record of their further collaboration. Is it possible that their falling out was directly the result of Thorpe's activities in 1609?

It is an intriguing possibility that Jonson was planning to publish *his* complete poems in direct response to the *SONNETS*, and in his dedication was making a direct comment on Thorpe's dedication, with its reference to his patron, and the possible concealment of its author's true identity. "I call you by your proper title, my Lord," says Jonson, "and *I* have no need to hide my own." If the chronology holds up, then Jonson's words assume a pivotal role in this story, as the first reference to the dedication as *a cypher*.

• • •

The puzzles that attend the *SONNETS* are clear. It has been seen why it is so strange that these poems, by such an author, should provoke so little in the way of discussion or debate at the time of first publishing. With the second, Benson edition, we have seen how another publisher could take that same material and fashion a product that would make a more substantial impact, and how uncharacteristic it would be for Thomas Thorpe, Ben Jonson's chosen publisher, to blunder his way into print with an edition wholly unsuited to its time and audience.

Finally, there are the puzzles of the dedication. If Thorpe was addressing either of the earls Herbert or Wriothesley, how could he get away with such an impertinent appellation, or the suggestion that they were involved in a homosexual relationship with the author? If he was addressing Shake-speare, what does "our ever-living poet" mean? And why not spell the author's name out, or at least spell it correctly? If some other person was meant, why be secretive? Most of all, why did Thorpe depart so completely from his usual over-emphatic and exuberant style?

Metaphorically, the explanations surrounding the publication of the *SONNETS* resemble the pre-Copernican theories of the cosmos. As astronomical observations in the Middle Ages became increasingly detailed, so the orbits of the heavenly bodies were presumed to be ever more exotic in order to keep the fundamental theory of the Earth-centred universe intact. In the case of the *SONNETS*, the more evidence one assembles, the more it seems one's explanations must loop-the-loop and spiral back on themselves if they are to accommodate both what Thorpe must have been aware of, and yet would not, or could not explicitly state in his dedication.

But the dedication exists. And the puzzles that attend it are real. In Part Two, the evidence will be presented that the *SONNETS* dedication is indeed—as Jonson perhaps hinted—a brilliantly executed cypher revealing that the sonnets were written, not by the Stratford player, William Shaksper, but by Edward de Vere, 17th Earl of Oxford. This hypothesis is, of course, not new. But equally, when Galileo first witnessed the moons of Jupiter, the heliocentric theory of Copernicus had been around for nearly a century. What Galileo presented was the *proof*.

II. REVELATIONS

The Authorship Debate, encompassing the various theories that the works published under the name of "Shake-speare" were written, not by the Stratford-born actor/manager William Shaksper but by someone else, is a many-headed monster. The internet has spawned hundreds of chat rooms and forums where devotees dissect the esoteric extremities of their candidate's case. As a result, most academics who have devoted their energy, and career, to studying the works of Shake-speare steer an exasperated course to avoid the clutches of its writhing tentacles. Jonathan Bate sums up the frustration:

> "Sometimes it is suspected that the academics
> are covering up a scandal: it is said that *we*
> *do not know* who wrote the plays attributed to
> Shakespeare. Every now and then—it has been
> happening for over a hundred years—an amateur
> literary sleuth comes forward and, amidst a flurry
> of publicity, claims to have solved the mystery.
> The professors are likened to the plodding
> Inspector Lestrade; the truth can only be revealed
> by some unacknowledged Sherlock Holmes."

The problem for the establishment is a simple one. There is no manuscript document, or even printed document, in which Shaksper the player confirms that he is the author of any single work of the Shake-speare canon. Regardless of how significant a fact one considers this to be, it is nonetheless a fact. If only such a "Rosetta Stone" existed, there would be no Authorship Debate. It is as simple as that. In the absence of such a text, the author of the canon could, logically speaking, be anyone. And in this, Bate is being slightly disingenuous. For in absolute terms, the "academics" (and we have to suppose by this he means "those who know best") do not *know* who wrote the plays attributed to Shake-speare. Or, for that matter, the poems.

Anyone—amateur or otherwise—who wishes to remain oblivious to the brain-numbing complexities of the Authorship Debate, should certainly avoid John Michell's entertaining 1996 book *Who Wrote Shakespeare?*. In this compendium of Authorship controversies, Michell drily elaborates the arguments for a number of the central and peripheral candidates for the title of True Author of the Works of the Bard. That there are many puzzles cannot be denied, says Michell, though as to their merits, he stays mostly, and even-handedly, on the fence. In relation to the sonnets, however, he does go so far as to venture an opinion. "On the balance of evidence it seems reasonable to guess" he concludes, that the sonnets were written by Edward de Vere, 17th Earl of Oxford.

Born in 1550 into one of the most ancient earldoms of England, de Vere was in many respects the model of the Renaissance courtier. His father's death resulted in the 12-year-old earl being raised as a Royal Ward in the household of the Queen's closest advisor, Sir William Cecil, later Lord Burghley. There, he was tutored by some of the finest minds of the day and had the run of one of the most extensive libraries in Europe. It was to that very library, it will be remembered, that Burghley added Dr John Dee's gift of Trithemius's manual of cryptography, *Steganographia* in 1563. Much to the delight, perhaps, of his inquisitive 13-year-old ward.

A gifted scholar, de Vere graduated from Cambridge at 14, received an MA from Oxford at 16, and entered Gray's Inn to study law at age 17. By this time he was skilled in the translation of Latin and Greek, wrote poetry extensively and had a coterie of friends among whom many were poets that he subsidised financially and who dedicated many of their own works to him. He was a highly skilled horseman, fond of hunting with hawks and hounds and was considered exceptional at jousting. In 1571, he was wedded to

Burghley's daughter, Anne (after her father's ennoblement sanctioned the union between a commoner and a peer), and in a tempestuous marriage they had three daughters before her death in 1588. In the 1580s, as well as taking military commands in the Netherlands and during the Armada campaign, de Vere maintained both adult and children's acting companies in London.

Throughout his adult life, de Vere's two principal concerns were money, and his Queen. The former he had almost entirely run out of by the 1580s, partly through his own profligacy and partly through the machinations of the acquisitive Lord Burghley. His relationship with the Virgin Queen was complex, intensely personal and ultimately, a source of great sadness to him.

The eleven-year-old de Vere first met the newly-crowned Elizabeth in 1561, when the Queen and her travelling Court paid a six-day visit to his family home at Castle Hedingham in Essex. Later he would become for a time perhaps her closest favourite, to the extent that it has been suggested they may have become lovers. Political infighting then turned their friendship to hostility for a time, exacerbated by an affair the still-married de Vere brazenly conducted with one of Elizabeth's Maids of Honour, Ann Vavasour, which resulted in an illegitimate son, also christened Edward. Though their relationship never seems to have recovered from the blows it sustained during this period in the late 1580s, Elizabeth held sufficient affection for her "Turk" as she called de Vere, to grant him a life-supporting annual allowance of £1,000, and permission to marry another of her closest companions, Elizabeth Trentham, in 1591, with whom he had a son, Henry, in 1593.

In 1597, with mixed feelings about his "banishment", de Vere retired from the Court to a manor house in Hackney with his family. His known correspondence until his death mainly concerns his attempts to recover lands and titles lost during his younger years. On the occasion of the Queen's death in 1603, however, he wrote to Sir

Robert Cecil, son and heir of Lord Burghley, of his "great grief", in a manner aptly summing up his perspective on their relationship, and indeed on life in general:

> In this common shipwreck, mine is above
> all the rest, who least regarded, though often
> comforted, she hath left to try my fortune
> among the alterations of time and chance,
> either without sail whereby to take the
> advantage of any prosperous gale, or
> without anchor to ride till the storm be over.

He died the following year.

Many thousands of words have been written on the "evidence" that de Vere was the real author behind some or all of the Shake-speare plays. These "Oxfordian" arguments rely on matching up events in de Vere's life to details in the writings of Shake-speare and claiming that the correspondences are so strong as to "prove" de Vere was Shake-speare. Indeed, the number and extent of these correspondences has left de Vere as by far the most popular anti-Stratfordian candidate.

Those biographical arguments will not be rehearsed here. There are now several biographies available of "de Vere as Shake-speare" that elaborate this evidence, and while such accounts are interesting in their different ways, all suffer from the same weakness. Without documentary proof to establish their premise—that de Vere *is* Shake-speare—the piling of biographical coincidences on top of one another achieves little. For even supposing, say, that the life of Edward de Vere matches in a thousand particulars the journey of Hamlet, we need conclude no more than that *Hamlet* is a play about a man very like Edward de Vere; there is no compulsion to infer that Edward de Vere also wrote it.

In relation to the Authorship Debate, the case of the sonnets differs from that of the plays in that the puzzles which surround their publication are not now, and never have been, the sole preserve of the anti-Stratfordians. Indeed, the entire discussion of this book so far has been based solely on the work of Stratfordian scholars, who certainly accept the puzzles exist, even if they deny that they have any bearing on who wrote the poems. That every edition of the sonnets devotes a large part of its introduction to these questions, and that so few of them agree on the best way to answer them, is itself testament to the enigma.

What follows demonstrates beyond reasonable doubt that the *SONNETS* dedication is precisely the Rosetta Stone that all sides in the Authorship Debate have been waiting for. The reason it has not been established as such until now is twofold. Firstly, all the known evidence has not been assembled in one place before. Secondly, some evidence has been overlooked by previous accounts, or has remained entirely hidden until now. There are several pieces of the jigsaw, that together provide an overwhelming case that the dedication was a deliberate exercise in wordplay and concealment, conclusively demonstrating that Edward de Vere was the author of the sonnets, and a great deal more.

Anyway, on with the deerstalker and out with the meerschaum pipe.

The first cypher

In 1999, John M Rollett published a paper entitled *Secrets of the Dedication to Shake-speare's Sonnets*, in which he claimed to have discovered three coded messages in the *SONNETS* dedication. In the first of these messages, Rollett argues, Thomas Thorpe directly names the Edward de Vere as the author of the sonnets.

His suspicions were aroused by the layout of the dedication, particularly the unusual use of full stops after each word. It is usually supposed that these marks are intended to give the dedication the appearance of a Roman inscription, as a similar device was used by Jonson and Thorpe in *Sejanus*. Rollett wondered, however, if the full stops might indicate something more: that the number of words in the dedication was important in some way. Seeking some other clue that might provide a key with which to unlock that code, Rollett lighted upon the peculiar typographical presentation of the dedication in three unequal triangles, of six lines, two lines and four lines:

TO.THE.ONLIE.BEGETTER.OF.
THESE.INSVING.SONNETS.
Mr.W.H. ALL.HAPPINESSE.
AND.THAT.ETERNITIE.
PROMISED.
BY.

OVR.EVER-LIVING.POET.
WISHETH.

THE.WELL-WISHING.
ADVENTVRER. IN
SETTING.
FORTH.

Straight away he saw a coincidence:

EDWARD	DE	VERE
6	2	4

As Rollett pointed out, there is a contemporary reference for this association of the letters of de Vere's name and verse lines. The source is a poem by the poet, playwright, Queen's messenger and sometime spy, Anthony Munday (1560–1633). At an early point in his career, Munday had a close association of patronage, and possibly employment, with de Vere, and dedicated a number of publications to him. In particular, in 1588, Munday published a collection of lyrics entitled, *A Banqvet of Daintie Conceits,* the dedication of which commences:

> E xcept I should in friendship seem ingrate,
> D enying duty, whereto I am bound;
> W ith letting slip your Honour's worthy state,
> A t all assays, which I have noble found,
> R ight well I might refrain to handle pen:
> D enouncing aye the company of men.
>
> D own, dire despair, let courage come in Place,
> E xalt his fame whom Honour doth embrace.
>
> V irtue hath aye adorn'd your valiant heart,
> E xampl'd by your deeds of lasting fame:
> R egarding such as take God Mars his part
> E ach where by proof, in honour and in name.

Such acrostic poems were common at the time (Jonson was fond of them too), and so the principle would be familiar to any poet of the day. Wondering if the 6-2-4 sequence might be a *key* unlocking a code, Rollett counted from the beginning of the dedication—six words, then two words, then four words. The result was coincidence number two:

TO.THE.ONLIE.BEGETTER.OF.
THESE.INSVING.SONNETS.
Mr.W.H. ALL.HAPPINESSE.
AND.THAT.ETERNITIE.
PROMISED.
BY.

OVR.EVER-LIVING.POET.

"These... sonnets... all... by... ever"

Interpreting "EVER" as an anagram of "Vere" or as representing "E Ver" (the family name is thought to originate from Ver in the Bessin region of Normandy), the author's assertion seems as simple as it is startling: the sonnets are by de Vere.

There is also a contemporary precedent for this association of de Vere's name with the word "ever". In an early poem attributed to de Vere, and subtitled on the manuscript "Ann Vavasour's Echo" he played on the rhymes and coincidences of "ever" and "Vere", thus:

Oh heavens ! who was the first that bred in me this fever? Vere.
Who was the first that gave the wound whose fear I wear for ever? Vere.
What tyrant, Cupid, to my harm usurps thy golden quiver? Vere.
What sight first caught this heart and can from bondage it deliver? Vere.

The first cypher and the key that reveals it are simpler, more direct and less ambiguous than any other of the supposed secret messages presented as evidence in the Authorship Debate. Nevertheless, if they were the only coincidences it would be reasonable to dispute them as freak occurrences—albeit surprising ones. There is also a weakness in the argument, as Rollett saw it, in that for the 6-2-4 key to be accepted, it ought to apply to the whole dedication. Rollett thought that it did not. The message, he said, "started off in quite an interesting fashion, but sadly it ended up as rubbish." Interestingly, Rollett did not go on to give the "message" in full, and in later years he decided to back another candidate as the author, which led to him losing faith in his discovery altogether.

But Rollett was premature in discounting his finding. Applying the 6-2-4 rule to the whole dedication reveals the following text:

TO.THE.ONLIE.BEGETTER.OF.

THESE.INSVING.SONNETS.

Mr.W.H. ALL.HAPPINESSE.

AND.THAT.ETERNITIE.

PROMISED.

BY.

OVR.EVER-LIVING.POET.

WISHETH.

THE.WELL-WISHING.

ADVENTVRER. IN

SETTING.

FORTH.

"These... sonnets... all... by... ever... the... forth"

It is these last two words that provoked Rollett's doubts, and led him to stick to his shorter and weaker version of the message. The absence of an adequate explanation of the phrase "the forth", clearly undermines the overall case, and no credible suggestion of how these words might fit into the picture has so far been given.

What might "the forth" conceivably mean? An obvious suggestion is that it is a cypher-maker's approximation for "the fourth", which is well within the bounds of interpretation, given the flexibility of spelling in that period. Unfortunately, there is no straightforward association of the de Vere as being "the fourth" *of* anything.

To date, the closest anyone has come to an explanation is the suggestion that de Vere was, by dint of peculiarities of succession, only the fourth of the Earls of Oxford to be styled "Viscount Bolebec". While it is certainly true that de Vere was known as Viscount Bolebec, whether he was the fourth Oxford to be so-called is all but impossible to establish. In truth, it seems unlikely, given that the Bolebec inheritance began with Robert, the 3rd Earl, in the early 1200s, and even *Cokayne's Complete Peerage of England*, that touchstone of ancestral lineages, can do little more than speculate which of the earls subsequently adopted the self-styled title (it was never officially created).

To make the strongest case that the message is deliberate, an explanation is certainly required. Fortunately there is one, and it is remarkably simple—so simple it is surprising it has not been pointed out before.

One of the features that characterise the early life of de Vere, especially in relation to Queen Elizabeth, was a repeated desire to be allowed to command a military force, in order to demonstrate what at the time was considered one of the crowning attributes of nobility: martial prowess. In November 1569, the 19-year-old earl petitioned the Queen, via her closest advisor, his own guardian, Lord Burghley, to be allowed to join the expeditionary forces in the Netherlands, where Protestant insurgents had been waging war against the occupying power, Spain, since the late 1560s. As can be seen from his letter, it wasn't the first time of asking:

Having no other means whereby to speak with you myself,
I am bold to impart my mind in paper, earnestly desiring your

Lordship that at this instant as heretofore you have given me your good word to have me see the wars and services in strange and foreign places, sithe you could not then obtain me licence of the Queen's Majesty, now you will do me so much honor as that by your purchase of my licence I may be called to the service of my prince and country as at this present troublous time a number are...

His determination was perhaps not surprising. The war of independence that was begun in this period dominated English foreign policy well into the next century. By the time King James came to the throne in 1603, if they had not served in the Low Countries themselves, every man would know a family member or friend who had. But in the 1570s, though the liberation of the Netherlands from Spanish dominion was a cause unofficially supported by Elizabeth, she declined to let the young Earl of Oxford participate.

In 1572, de Vere petitioned Burghley again, pleading:

If there were any service to be done abroad, I had rather serve there than at home, where yet some honour were to be got.

Once more the Queen refused, no doubt in part because England was still not officially involved in the Dutch struggle. Two years later, de Vere's impatience finally got the better of him, and he simply absconded across the channel for a brief foray into Flanders, before his enraged Queen ordered him back. He was sufficiently chastened to remain obediently at home for the next ten years.

Everything changed, however, when in 1585 the fall of Antwerp forced the English hand. On 20 August that year, Elizabeth signed the Treaty of Nonsuch, and England went to war against Spain on the Netherlands' behalf. Four days later, as one of the first wave of English commanders, de Vere was on route across the channel again, bound for Arnhem. His service in the Low Countries was brief, however. By June of 1586, whether by his own volition this time or not, he was back in England.

Though de Vere's military involvement in the war was curtailed, his family name would become synonymous with the greatest martial exploits that would eventually lead to the establishment of the independent Dutch republic. Leading English troops throughout the next 30 years were his two younger cousins, Francis and Horatio, the "Fighting Veres". Francis rose to the rank of Commander in Chief of the English forces, his younger brother Horatio followed him, and between them they orchestrated the most successful years of the Dutch campaigns, leading to the truce with Spain in 1609. As their 19th-century biographer Clements Markham put it: "In that fight no two names are so conspicuous ... The brother warriors stand out prominently as the representatives of their race in the great fight for freedom. They never faltered, never grew weary, but faithfully and loyally devoted their lives to a cause which is dear to all English-speaking people."

The association of the name of de Vere with the Low Countries conflict through Francis, Horatio and, briefly Edward from the 1580s until the 1620s, was inescapable. Who in the Netherlands would not know that "de Vere" was synonymous with the English commitment to the struggle for Dutch independence? Conversely, how many in England would appreciate the pun (and our third coincidence)—that "the forth" or "the fourth" translated into Dutch, is "de Vierde"?

If the author of the dedication was playing a game, combining hidden references to de Vere and an overt or "innocent" text, it would make perfect sense, when puzzling out the latter stages of the dedication, that the thought might have struck him to do double service with the phrase "the forth" and have a little joke to boot:

These sonnets all by E Ver de Vierde

It hardly needs pointing out that "de Vierde" is an anagram of "Ed de Vier". One could even claim that if "fourth" (*vierde*) and "four" (*vier*) were plausibly interchangeable in the early-17th-century context, the message might be construed as "Ever de Vier". But the remarkableness of the coincidence is apparent without these additional steps.

In sum, the "de Vierde" translation cypher means that there is a straightforward derivation of the whole phrase, and an explanation of its meaning, all of which is directly connected to de Vere.

It is interesting to note that in its first manifestation, "these sonnets all by E Ver de Vier de", has a whiff of the tongue-twister about it, encouraging the suspicion that the author is enjoying himself much more than is allowed by those who normally look for deep and serious motivations in their Shake-speare cyphers. It is a witty pun on the name—rather than a desperate attempt to communicate to posterity.

It is also worth noting that this first encryption is simple. There are many books, papers, and websites offering complex and ingenious explanations of the supposed hidden messages in Shake-speare's plays and poems. Among the most prolific are those arguing that Sir Francis Bacon, the great philosopher/scientist, wrote the Shake-speare canon, or organised its writing, as part of a plan to provide a complete philosophical system for the dawning of a New Age of man. There are other, more recent theories relating encryptions thought to demonstrate that the plays are from the hand of the nobleman and proto-republican politician Sir Henry Neville.

In all these accounts, a great number of words are expended on the issue of what was at stake in the concealment of the true identity of the author. The gravity of the enterprise, it is suggested, requires great secrecy. The terrible consequences of discovery make necessary complex levels of meaning and esoteric reference systems—Rosicrucian and Kabbalistic symbolism for example—to conceal their proof that Bacon, or Neville, wrote the plays.

As was discussed in the first part of this book, it is certain that secrecy and code-making were a hugely significant part of communication in this period and that the techniques used were highly sophisticated. But what is not usually explained by the proponents of the various theories is why, if the stakes were really so high, the secret authors left clues to their identity at all. Why not just remain secret? The resulting paradox creates the need to justify an uncomfortable tension in the psyche of the author, where the desire to remain hidden constantly wrestles with the urge to be revealed.

In contrast to that motive of obsessive secrecy, the first cypher above appears to indicate absolutely the reverse. The key to revealing the message—the arrangement of lines in a 6-2-4 pattern—could not be more plainly on view. The "hidden" message, with its "forth/vierde" punning, seems playful rather than earnest. Rather than being desperately intent on a crusade to tell the world the "truth" about the sonnets, we might instead imagine this author looking for interesting and entertaining solutions to the word puzzle he was creating. It is as if that author fully expects a sharp-eyed reader to get the joke, and the air of witty mischief is palpable. As we proceed, this playful air will be a repeating theme.

For the moment, let's just say that whatever the motive of the author, in logical terms the case is strong that this first cypher was deliberately written into the dedication. The 6-2-4 key suggested by the layout both directly relates to the name Edward de Vere, and also reveals a message *about* Edward de Vere. It seems unlikely that one of the most controversial texts in the Shake-speare canon should contain a message of this kind, that points directly to the primary alternative candidate in the Authorship Debate.

If this were the extent of the evidence, the case might be considered interesting, but inconclusive. But this is just the beginning, and the coincidences only become more extraordinary.

The second cypher

Consider the layout of the dedication again, in particular, the prominence of the line "our ever-living poet":

TO.THE.ONLIE.BEGETTER.OF.
THESE.INSVING.SONNETS.
Mr.W.H. ALL.HAPPINESSE.
AND.THAT.ETERNITIE.
PROMISED.
BY.

OVR.EVER-LIVING.POET.
WISHETH.

THE.WELL-WISHING.
ADVENTVRER. IN
SETTING.
FORTH.

It will be remembered from Part One that there is considerable disagreement over the interpretation of this phrase. Does it perhaps refer to an unnamed writer such as Virgil or Spenser, or perhaps to God? The central problem, of course, is that in that period the phrase was nowhere used to describe a living person. However, if, as we have seen, the author of the dedication believes de Vere to be the author of the sonnets, this difficulty vanishes. Indeed, the phrase becomes singularly appropriate. In May 1609, de Vere had been dead almost five years. Little is known about his death, other than its date, 24 June 1604, and it is usually supposed that having suffered ill-health for a number of years, he fell victim to the vicious plague outbreak of 1603–4. Thus, the simplest reading of "our ever-living poet" as meaning "the dead, but immortal, author" fits well.

However, apart from being apposite in de Vere's case, there is also something provocative in the way that the phrase "our ever-living poet" is placed so brazenly in the middle of the layout. If the first cypher is accepted, then the word "ever" was very specifically placed as the 20th word in the sequence. The other words of the line in which it appears could be different, as long as the number remained the same. Yet this line stands proud as if deliberately trumpeting the author's name beyond merely alluding to him as deceased. Is there a reason why this might be? As John Michell pointed out, there certainly is. The following entry in *The Principal, Historical, and Allusive Arms, Borne by Families of the United Kingdom*, of 1803, gives it away:

The phrase "our ever-living" is an anagram of the de Vere family motto "vero nil verius"—"nothing truer than truth". Almost.

The keen-eyed will spot that the anagram is only exact if the terminal "G" is exchanged for an "S". However, before a plea in mitigation for this discrepancy is offered, consider the nature of this latest coincidence: the phrase "our ever-living" is an almost exact anagram of the family motto of the very person we have just seen revealed as the author of the *SONNETS*. It is, of course, unlikely that the author would be tempted to write the phrase as "OUR EVER-LIVINS" just to make the anagram perfect, and it doesn't take much charity to allow that he might have felt he'd done well enough by changing one letter only. But there is an even stronger explanation of why the author would have considered the match to be, to all intents and purposes, exact.

The plea in mitigation is this. The manuscript for the dedication that Thorpe gave to his printer George Elde would certainly have been hand written. In the 16th and early 17th centuries, the most common formal writing was a standardised script known as "secretary hand". Here are examples, from a 16th-century handwriting manual, of a capital S in secretary hand:

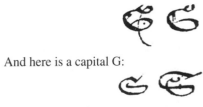

And here is a capital G:

Sorry, that's not right. The first one is the "G" and the second one is the "S". It's easy to get them mixed up. The point is clear: to the author, sitting at his desk composing the anagram with quill and ink, idly playing with the letters of the motto in secretary hand, swapping the two letters would be an instant and natural witticism. Where Jonathan Bate hopes for a dodgy proofreader mistaking "S" for "H" to give him his "Mr WH", in this case the entirely deliberate interchanging of similar letters gives us an exact anagram of de Vere's family motto, right in the middle of the dedication.

Again there is a striking sense that the author is amusing himself, and playing a game with his reader. And it was a game well known in contemporary circles. Anagramming is widely documented as a popular literary sport among writers of the period, even with its own well-defined rules. Most intriguingly, the exchange of letters suggests that the author may have originally expected the dedication to have been read as a handwritten manuscript and *not* in printed form.

To the pile of coincidences surrounding the first encrypted message, the appearance of the de Vere motto centre stage in the dedication can now be added:

TO.THE.ONLIE.BEGETTER.OF.
THESE.ENSUING.SONNETS.
MR.W.H.ALL.HAPPINESSE.
AND.THAT.ETERNITIE.
PROMISED.
BY.
VERO.NIL.VERIUS.POET.

This anagram cypher provides a satisfying explanation for all the puzzles enumerated in the first part of this book relating to the identity of "our ever-living poet". Firstly, Jonathan Bate is correct in that the phrase *is* intended to honour a poet who is dead—he is just wrong about which one. Secondly, the phrase names that poet as de Vere, via his motto. Thirdly, if the "ever-living poet" is the sonnets author—de Vere—then it is consistent that the "eternitie" being promised in the dedication is that lauded in the first 17 sonnets by their composer—that is, procreation. Fourthly, for completeness' sake, the phrase "our ever-living poet" can be interpreted as referring to God, *as well as de Vere*, without contradiction of the other meanings.

Thus, four simple words that spawn endless contradictions if the author is assumed to be the Stratford player, transmute into a glittering multi-layered pun on the name of the author of the poems, Edward de Vere. Not a bad return on investment. But as will now be seen, the author of the dedication was just getting warmed up.

The transposition cyphers

The first hidden message in the dedication is an ingenious development of a cypher invented and introduced into Elizabethan society by the Italian mathematician, philosopher, professional gambler and cryptographer Jerome Cardano. An astrologer by trade, in the 1550s Cardano was certainly in London, where he prepared a horoscope for the young King Edward, and was counted among the close circle of Dr John Dee. One of his cyphers, which became known in its various forms as the Cardano Grille, was used to conceal a secret message inside another "innocent" text. By placing a piece of card or paper with holes cut into it over the innocent text, the hidden message would be revealed through the apertures. It's the stuff of many a youngster's spy game.

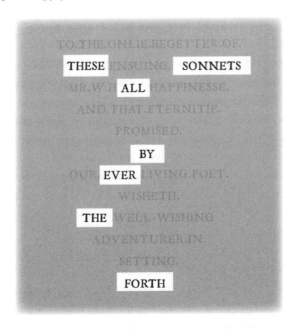

Although the first message concealed in the dedication cypher can be revealed using a grille such as the above, in this case the author adapted the basic form and included the key to revealing the message—6-2-4—within the layout of the dedication, making the grille unnecessary, and the cypher much easier to crack. Intriguingly, the next cyphers we will examine are also variations of the Cardano Grille, which suggests that the author might have been familiar with the work of the Italian logician.

Another method of constructing a Cardano Grille is to take a square or rectangular grid, and write one's secret message vertically in the columns. The remaining spaces are then filled with letters to create an innocent text, which when written out in sentence form effectively conceals the secret. To reveal the hidden message, the text is written out again in the appropriate grid and the message reappears.

Inspired by his initial discovery, Rollett began experimenting by placing the text of the dedication in grids of different sizes. Counting the letters of the dedication, he found it to contain 144—a perfect square. Disappointingly, however, in a grid of 12 columns and 12 rows he found nothing resembling a message of any kind.

Rollett persevered, increasing the number of columns one by one, and in a grid of 15 columns across, he found something interesting:

T	O	T	H	E	O	N	L	I	E	B	E	G	E	T
T	E	R	O	F	T	H	E	S	E	I	N	S	U	I
N	G	S	O	N	N	E	T	S	M	R	W	H	A	L
L	H	A	P	P	I	N	E	S	S	E	A	N	D	T
H	A	T	E	T	E	R	N	I	T	I	E	P	R	O
M	I	S	E	D	B	Y	O	U	R	E	V	E	R	L
I	V	I	N	G	P	O	E	T	W	I	S	H	E	T
H	T	H	E	W	E	L	L	W	I	S	H	I	N	G
A	D	V	E	N	T	U	R	E	R	I	N	S	E	T
T	I	N	G	F	O	R	T	H

Unsurprisingly, Rollett recognised "Henry" as Wriothesley, one of the main candidates for the Fair Youth of the sonnets. An encryption of the identity of this elusive character would be a discovery indeed. But what are the chances, Rollett wondered, of a five-letter name turning up in one of the 144 grids obtainable from a text of this length? He calculated the odds at about 1 in 1,000. Not hugely unlikely.

Encouraged, however, Rollett pressed on, and in a perfect rectangular grid consisting of 18 columns by 8 rows he hit what seemed to be the jackpot:

```
T O T H E O N L I E B E G E T T E R
O F T H E S E I N S U I N G S O N N
E T S M R W H A L L H A P P I N E S
S E A N D T H A T E T E R N I T I E
P R O M I S E D B Y O U R E V E R L
I V I N G P O E T W I S H E T H T H
E W E L L W I S H I N G A D V E N T
U R E R I N S E T T I N G F O R T H
```

Rollett's second "transposition" cypher, reading down-up-down in three separate pieces, tantalisingly reads "Wr+ioth+esley". An accident of chance? Rollett estimated the odds of these three segments turning up in one of the grids at 1 in 20,000. Combined with the "Henry" odds, this puts the probability of any five- and 11-letter forename/surname combination turning up in two of the grids at 1 in 20 million.

These are now pretty long odds, but Rollett went further and suggested that the odds of not just *any* such name turning up, but the *main candidate* for the Fair Youth, must be longer still. Putting "a very vague figure" on the probability at 1 in 100, Rollett estimated the likelihood of these two names appearing by chance as 1 in 2 billion. At this point, Rollett rested his case.

When considering the broken pieces of the WRIOTHESLEY cypher, it is important to bear in mind that, including the innocent message, the author of the dedication is now fitting together *five* messages into the dedication. Juggling the text to make all the pieces mesh would obviously require a high level of linguistic ingenuity, and a good deal of patience. And the person for whom they were intended would no doubt be delighted and impressed by that ingenuity, in concealing not only the identity of the poet, but also the chief subject of his poems.

Nonetheless, if these five messages represented the limits of that ingenuity, we might marvel at the coincidences, but *still* perhaps doubt that the cyphers are really there as a result of anything more than the operation of blind chance. But there is more to come. If Rollett had pursued his instincts a little further, he would have laid all doubts to rest.

Further discoveries

The 18 by 8 perfect rectangle grid has much more to reveal than Rollett supposed. What he failed to observe was this:

T	O	T	H	E	O	N	L	I	E	B	E	G	E	T	T	E	R
O	F	T	H	E	S	E	I	N	S	U	I	N	G	S	O	N	N
E	T	S	M	R	W	H	A	L	L	H	A	P	P	I	N	E	S
S	E	A	N	D	T	H	A	T	E	T	E	R	N	I	T	I	E
P	R	O	M	I	S	E	D	B	Y	O	U	R	E	V	E	R	L
I	V	I	N	G	P	O	E	T	W	I	S	H	E	T	H	T	H
E	W	E	L	L	W	I	S	H	I	N	G	A	D	V	E	N	T
U	R	E	R	I	N	S	E	T	T	I	N	G	F	O	R	T	H

The transposition grid clearly contains a whole sentence looping around Wriothesley's name:

TO ESPIE OFT WR+IOTH+ESLEY WIT
NEED NOT HERE TRIE

Which we might expand and modernise slightly as: "To see Wriothesley often in these sonnets is easy if you use your wits."

It seems legitimate at this point to abandon discussion of probabilities. This nine-word sentence appears in a perfect rectangle, reads left to right, is grammatical—and grammatically complex— and is spelled correctly. The form of the words "espie", "oft" and "trie" is of course precisely what one would anticipate in an early 17th-century text.

The ramifications of the full WRIOTHESLEY cypher are significant. The extent of the message takes it beyond conjecture into the realms of being the first documentary proof that, unless the author of the dedication was lying, Wriothesley *was* the primary subject of the sonnets. This in itself is a remarkable discovery, as important to Stratfordians as to their opponents. Regardless of who one believes the author of the sonnets to have been, this new piece of evidence is certainly important.

Finally, the WRIOTHESLEY cypher is so clearly not a coincidence as to be tantamount to proof that the author *is* encrypting messages in the dedication. As such, it adds considerable support to the validity of the other cyphers we have already considered. I would suggest that it puts the burden of proof on those who deny the validity of those cyphers, since the WRIOTHESLEY cypher demonstrates that every word in the dedication was chosen with the utmost precision.

It now ought to be beyond doubt that the author of the dedication is playing a fantastically clever word game. And witty too, the tone of this latest cypher is once again playful—hide and seek. The encypherer loves word puzzles, and expects his reader to like them too. But if any doubts do remain as to his extraordinary skill in providing the recipient of the *SONNETS* with ever-more ingenious riddles to unravel, what follows puts the matter conclusively beyond doubt. Because, like any showman worth his salt, the author saved his best tricks for last.

The third transposition cypher

It was because I was so surprised both by the discovery of the full WRIOTHESLEY cypher and Rollett's failure to notice it, that I decided to look through the complete set of 144 transposition grids myself. If something that crucial could be missed, I thought, might something else have been? So it was that I ended up one June evening staring blurrily at grid after grid when, working across a grid composed of 25 columns and six rows, a striking sentence-like sequence of words leaped out:

LET... ROSIE... LIP... APE... OWN...

The word "ROSIE" in particular had an air of familiarity, and taking another look, I noticed something else that definitely rang bells. On the grid, the words "lip" and "ape" were connected to the word "poet" of the innocent message:

Including the word "poet" as part of the message gave:

LET ROSIE LIP POET APE OWN

Could it be, I wondered, a direct reference to *On Poet-Ape*—the satirical swipe from the pen of Ben Jonson encountered in Part One— that has been interpreted as a possible attack on Globe shareholder and player, Shaksper? Here it is again, this time in full.

On Poet-Ape

Poor POET-APE, that would be thought our chief,
Whose works are e'en the frippery of wit,
From brokage is become so bold a thief,
As we, the robb'd, leave rage, and pity it.
At first he made low shifts, would pick and glean,
Buy the reversion of old plays ; now grown
To a little wealth, and credit in the scene,
He takes up all, makes each man's wit his own :
And, told of this, he slights it. Tut, such crimes
The sluggish gaping auditor devours ;
He marks not whose 'twas first : and after-times
May judge it to be his, as well as ours.
Fool ! as if half eyes will not know a fleece
From locks of wool, or shreds from the whole piece ?

Jonson's target was clearly someone who was presenting the plays of others under his own name. Not only that, but Jonson makes no bones about the fact that the Poet-ape believes he is, or presents himself as, the *chief* of playwrights. What is interesting about Jonson's response is that while the Poet-ape's deception is apparently transparent to all and sundry, he is nonetheless getting away with it. In a period of intensely competitive struggle for writers to survive and defend their reputation and copyright, Jonson is stating that the one writer who thinks himself preeminent is a fraud, *and everyone knows it*. That Jonson, renowned for his intolerance of dishonesty and his willingness to "name and shame" his contemporaries, made no other reference to the identity of this most extravagant fraudster tempts the conclusion that this Poet-ape must have been protected— well protected—from open criticism.

However, there is a prior, and related, significance of the term Poet-ape. Though the term "ape" was commonly used in the period to refer to anyone who feigned abilities or attributes they did not possess, the specific pejorative "Poet-ape" was coined in a work entitled the *Defense of Poesie* by the revered courtier and poet Sir Philip Sidney, who was killed in the Netherlands in 1586 at the age of just 31. In what might be considered the first literary manifesto, written around 1581, Sidney used the term "Poet-ape" just once, towards his conclusion. Lamenting the forlorn reputation of English poetic writing, he remarked that:

> ...the cause why it is not esteemed in England,
> is the fault of Poet-apes, not Poets.

His target was the new breed of writers for the stage:

> But I have lavished out too many words of this play
> matter; I do it, because, as they are excelling parts
> of poesy, so is there none so much used in England,
> and none can be more pitifully abused; which, like an
> unmannerly daughter, showing a bad education, causeth
> her mother Poesy's honesty to be called in question.

The *Defense of Poesie* was not published until 1595, when it may well have been the spark that ignited the War of the Theatres in which Jonson and his fellow poets traded literary—and physical—blows, and which inspired Jonson to immortalise the Poet-ape in his epigram shortly thereafter.

If the message is genuine, then, the author of the dedication seems to be suggesting a relation either of *ownership* or *acknowledgement* between a Poet-ape—whether Jonson's or Sidney's—and "rosie lip". The answer clearly depends on whether "rosie lip" has a meaning that makes sense of whole. But what on earth does "rosie lip" refer to? The familiar-sounding word "rosie" had jumped out at me because of its period spelling, which echoed "espie" and "trie" in the WRIOTHESLEY cypher. Furthermore, being related to the word "rose", I wondered if there was a connection to Bate's suggestion of a play on the pronunciation of Wriothesley as "Roseley". I supposed "rosie" would be a pretty common occurrence in the literature of the time. But the phrase "rosie *lip*" — how common would that be, and if it did occur, would it help establish this as another genuine cypher?

I searched for the phrase in the complete works of Shake-speare. Online editions make this a very simple procedure nowadays, and the search engine took only a fraction of a second to return the result. It was, I'm sure, the closest I will ever come to knowing how Galileo felt on first sighting those pinpricks of light dancing in the darkness around Jupiter. For the phrase "rosie lip" *does* occur in Shake-speare's writing. Just once. In one of the sonnets.

116.

L et me not to the marriage of true mindes
Admit impediments, love is not love
Which alters when it alteration findes,
Or bends with the remover to remove.
O no, it is an ever fixed marke
That lookes on tempests and is never shaken;
It is the star to every wandring barke,
Whose worths unknowne, although his higth be taken.
Lov's not Times foole, though ROSIE LIPs and cheeks
Within his bending sickles compasse come,
Love alters not with his breefe houres and weekes,
But beares it out even to the edge of doome:
If this be error and upon me proved,
I never writ, nor no man ever loved.

This is the only appearance (my capitals of course) of the phrase "rosie lip" in the entire Shake-speare canon. In one of the most famous sonnets: 116.

Given that "rosie lip" is associated with just one Shake-speare work, the fact that it turns up in a transposition grid of the dedication text *at all* might be considered astonishing. How remarkable is it then, that in a dedication seemingly riddled with cyphers revolving around the authorship of the sonnets, a message is hidden that asserts some kind of relationship between a "Poet-ape" (a term coined by Sidney and adopted by Jonson to refer to an inferior or even sham playwright) and (via a possible pun on Wriothesley's name) *precisely one of the sonnets*?

Combining not just one, but now *six* different messages in the dedication would require a great deal of ingenuity, so given that the reference to sonnet 116 is a unique one, it is natural to suppose that the author of the dedication chose it for a very specific reason; whatever the connection is to the Poet-ape, one would expect it to be exemplified by this particular sonnet. It has already been shown that the author of the dedication believes the sonnets to be de Vere's. Is he therefore using this cypher to further demonstrate that the target of Sidney and Jonson is *de Vere*? There are good reasons to believe he singled out sonnet 116 to make precisely this point.

The E Ver sonnet

If one were looking for internal clues in the sonnets that de Vere was their author, sonnet 116 is perhaps the number one choice. Back at the beginning of this story it will be remembered that it was the word "ever" that served as the starting point for our investigation: "ever" as the anagram of "Vere", or as "E Ver".

The four-letter string "ever" occurs on its own and as part of other words including "never", "every", "whenever", "fever" and so on, in 52 of the 154 sonnets. This is not surprising given that the poems so often touch on eternity and the extremes of emotional feeling. The distribution of occurrences is revealing, however. In one or another of its forms, "ever" appears singly in a total of 44 sonnets. It appears twice in six of them, three times in none of them, four times in one, and is used its maximum five times also in just one sonnet.

Sonnet 116.

It is also worth noting that the final couplet of this sonnet has aroused criticism amongst scholars. It has been suggested that the author's rhetorical extravagance over-reaches and crude bombast takes over in the final moments of an otherwise masterly poem. However, any charge of lack of seriousness on the part of the poet here is mitigated by the fact that if de Vere was its author, the final line signifies a deliberate, rather than accidental, excursion into ironic self-identification:

"I never writ, nor no man E Ver loved."

That the author was exercising his wit—perhaps at the expense of his finer poetic judgement—makes complete sense in this context.

The Pole star sonnet

Secondly, with its famous opening line, 116 is one of the most instantly recognisable of the sonnets. Its subject, love, is likened to an "ever fixed mark", which is in turn elaborated as "the star to every wandring barke". The *ever*-laden reference here is of course to the Pole star, the navigational waysign around which the heavens revolve. Although star references appear in a total of seven of the sonnets, only in sonnet 116 is the Pole star the central image.

The sentiment of the poem might be simply expressed thus: "If you are determined to marry," says the poet, "I will not stand in your way, but I myself, and my love, will remain unchanging as the Pole star." As Katherine Duncan-Jones puts it, the poet "sets up an ideal of true love as unaltered and unalterable, which he claims is embodied in himself—or in *his sonnet*" (my italics).

This striking identification of the poet, and indeed the sonnet, with the single star has a straightforward connection to de Vere. It is immediately apparent on page 56. The device of the single silver star, blazoned on the Oxford coat of arms, was an ancient de Vere emblem known as the family "badge". Whether born aloft on a standard, worn on the sleeve by his retinue, or as a label on his property, the badge was the logo by which an aristocrat would be best known to the wider population.

According to a legend related by the early 16th-century antiquary John Leland, the de Vere badge had its origins at the siege of Antioch in 1098, when:

> ... the night coming on in the chase of this battayle, and waxing dark, the Christians being four miles from Antioch, God willing the safety of the Christians, showed a white star or mullet of five points, on the Christian host, which to every man's sight did alight and arrest upon the standard of Aubrey de Vere, there shining excessively.

After leading his men to safety by means of this divine aid, Aubrey, 1st Earl of Oxford, adopted the single star as the de Vere badge. The symbol remained of importance, particularly in the chaos of the battlefield. Being simple and clearly identifiable, the silver star on the de Vere standard provided the "ever fixed mark" around which followers could rally. Is it merely a coincidence that the author of the dedication is directing the recipient to the only sonnet in which the poet chooses as the central metaphor de Vere's badge — the single star — and identifies himself and the poem with it?

• • •

These features of sonnet 116 seem to mark it out from the rest as conspicuously bearing the "signature" of de Vere. What is remarkable is that we did not arrive at sonnet 116 because we were looking for clues that de Vere is Shake-speare. That is to say, sonnet 116 does not have to bear the burden of proving that de Vere wrote the poems. We were *directed* to it by the phrase "rosie lip" concealed in the dedication. The implications of the ROSIE LIP cypher are straightforward. The author of the dedication seems to be asserting a relationship of *ownership* or *acknowledgement* between the Poet-ape and de Vere.

This can now be seen to mean one of three things. On the one hand, the connection could be that de Vere *is* Sidney's Poet-ape, and the direction to sonnet 116 is a riposte to Sidney's slur on playwright-poets in the *Defense of Poesie*, that is, "if Sidney insults playwrights he insults *de Vere!*" (more of this later). On the other hand, the cypher could mean that de Vere literally *owns* the Poet-ape. Thus, if Jonson's well-protected target in *On Poet-Ape* really was the Globe actor/manager Shaksper, the cypher would represent the first concrete evidence that Shaksper was operating as a frontman for de Vere.

Thirdly, and most appealingly of all, being something of a magician when it comes to multiplicity of meaning, the author may have intended the ROSIE LIP cypher to score a double hit against both opponents simultaneously.

Who wrote the dedication?

It is clear that the author of the dedication knew that de Vere wrote the sonnets and that their principal subject was Wriothesley. It seems likely that he also knew that the term Poet-ape had special significance with reference to Sidney or Jonson or both, and that sonnet 116—being loaded with self-references—was a particularly important poem for making clear the connection between de Vere and the Poet-ape. Such intimacy with the context of the poems implies that the author of the dedication was close to their source. The burning question is: who was he?

Not Thorpe, certainly. The reasoning for this is unambiguous. While the author of the dedication was clearly on a mission to pack as much information as possible about the sonnets, their inspiration, and the poet who wrote them, into those 144 characters, in 1609 this information was still personal and potentially embarrassing if put into the public domain.

Throughout this book, it has been argued that the encryption techniques being used are straightforward ones, and that their tone suggests that the author while being ingenious, was not being devious, but was rather demonstrating his intellectual prowess by constructing such a complex set of cyphers. However, humorous intentions notwithstanding, it is now clear that he would have also been aware that he was revealing an extremely close relationship, perhaps even a love affair, between de Vere, one of the most important earls of the recent past (whose wife, son and daughters were very much alive to be offended) and Henry Wriothesley, one of the most powerful earls then living. If that wasn't enough, there is also the small matter of de Vere's involvement with a mistress, the Dark Lady.

In 1609, when the sonnets manuscript came into his hands, there is no obvious motive for Thorpe to risk his reputation, his livelihood, possibly even his liberty, to reveal information about the sonnets from which he had absolutely nothing personally to gain. Even if he had the skill, the time and the intellectual energy to compose such a complex encryption revealing the connection between Shakespeare, de Vere and Wriothesley, and was bold enough to disregard the potential fallout, he could only expect to bring trouble his way by going ahead and doing it.

Crucially, supposing Thorpe did encrypt both de Vere's and Wriothesley's names into the dedication, the ROSIE LIP cypher is entirely redundant from Thorpe's point of view. Perhaps the most idiosyncratic and personally revelatory of the secret texts, this cypher reveals the author of the dedication as not only relishing his own ingenuity, but as being sufficiently offended by the Jonson/Sidney jibe to respond to it in this most direct, yet paradoxically, utterly indirect way, on de Vere's behalf. There is no obvious reason why Thorpe would be concerned to redress this particular insult to de Vere, when he had already so clearly identified him with Shakespeare on the title page of the *SONNETS* and by the first cypher "These sonnets all by E Ver".

Furthermore, even if Thorpe was sufficiently *au fait* with the content of the poems to know that the phrase "rosie lip" would direct the recipient of dedication to one sonnet, and one sonnet only, there is no obvious reason why he might expect the wider world to care about the Poet-ape slur five years after de Vere's death in 1604. Sidney's remark first became public property in 1595, and *On Poet-Ape* was probably composed not long after that, so the Poet-ape insult might be as many as 14 years old by 1609.

These considerations make Thorpe's authorship of the dedication, already unlikely, utterly inexplicable. And whoever the author really was, it is clear that he must have felt himself immune to any risk of incurring the displeasure of either the poet or the recipient of the poems. Via a short digression on the nature of transposition grids, the identity of that author can now be revealed.

The perfect rectangle

If a final demonstration of the genuineness of the transposition cyphers were needed, it can be shown that they appear in precisely the grids a cryptographer might be expected to use, given the number of letters in the dedication. The dedication text contains 144 characters, which means 144 grids are obtainable, from one with 144 columns and just one row through to a grid with a single column and 144 rows.

The WRIOTHESLEY cypher, it will be remembered, appears in a grid of 18 columns by 8 rows. That is, it appears in a *perfect rectangle*. Perfect rectangles are important if an encypherer wishes his secret texts to be discovered without too much difficulty. They are the first place the curious might look for transposition cyphers, if wishing to narrow down the search. Therefore, in attempting to conceal several messages simultaneously, it would make sense for the encypherer to stick to a small number of perfect rectangle grids corresponding to the number of messages he was attempting to combine. Manipulating the texts in these grids would still present a fearsome intellectual challenge, of course.

Of the 144 grids available, 15 are perfect rectangles:

COLUMNS			ROWS
144	x	1	
72	x	2	
48	x	3	
36	x	4	
24	x	6	
18	x	8	
16	x	9	
12	x	12	
9	x	16	
8	x	18	
6	x	24	
4	x	36	
3	x	48	
2	x	72	
1	x	144	

However, not all 15 grids are equally suitable for the task of concealing cyphers. To create each cypher, the author is faced with a blank grid in which he is simultaneously writing two messages. The first is the longer "innocent" text that runs horizontally across the grid (in this case "To the onlie begetter of...etc."). The second is the cypher text, the hidden message that runs vertically (for example, "To espie oft Wriothesley... etc.").

The principal difficulty lies in being able easily to scan both messages at the same time. In any grid with less than five rows, words in the vertical, secret, message will be almost impossible to read. For this reason only grids with more than five rows are suitable. This reduces the number of available perfect rectangle grids from 15 to the following 11:

COLUMNS	24	x	6	ROWS
	18	x	8	
	16	x	9	
	12	x	12	
	9	x	16	
	8	x	18	
	6	x	24	
	4	x	36	
	3	x	48	
	2	x	72	
	1	x	144	

Consider next the number of columns. The horizontal, innocent, message must run continuously from the top left to the bottom right through all the rows of the grid. Being long, it contains a large number of words, and most importantly it must be a meaningful statement. In grids that are wider than they are tall (ie those having more columns than rows) the innocent message scans easily and can be imagined in reasonably large stretches at a time. However, as the number of columns decreases and the grids become taller than they are wide (ie those having more rows than columns), it quickly becomes very difficult to assimilate the horizontal message. Going down the above list, by the time one reaches the grid of 16 rows by 9 columns, the horizontal message has become very difficult to read easily:

T	O	T	H	E	O	N	L	I
E	B	E	G	E	T	T	E	R
O	F	T	H	E	S	E	I	N
S	U	I	N	G	S	O	N	N
E	T	S	M	R	W	H	A	L
L	H	A	P	P	I	N	E	S
S	E	A	N	D	T	H	A	T
E	T	E	R	N	I	T	I	E
P	R	O	M	I	S	E	D	B
Y	O	U	R	E	V	E	R	L
I	V	I	N	G	P	O	E	T
W	I	S	H	E	T	H	T	H
E	W	E	L	L	W	I	S	H
I	N	G	A	D	V	E	N	T
U	R	E	R	I	N	S	E	T
T	I	N	G	F	O	R	T	H

For the encypherer, faced with a blank 16 by 9 grid, it would now present an extra challenge to go about imagining what words might be used to make the long horizontal message coherent. Not impossible of course, but off-putting. In the subsequent grids with fewer columns still, it is certainly all but impossible.

If this grid is ruled out, and also the grids with still fewer columns from the previous list, four perfect rectangle grids remain that would give the encypherer a reasonable chance of successfully combining several messages at the same time in the overall text. It can be seen that one of these grids does contain the WRIOTHESLEY cypher.

24	x	6	?
18	x	8	**TO ESPIE OFT WRIOTHESLEY**...
16	x	9	?
12	x	12	?

The HENRY cypher, it may be recalled, was not discovered in a perfect rectangle grid, but an irregular grid of 15 columns by 10 rows (page 60). However, as Rollett pointed out in his paper, if one increases the number of columns by one, the name does appear in a perfect rectangle of 16 columns and 9 rows:

T	O	T	H	E	O	N	L	I	E	B	E	G	E	T	T
E	R	O	F	T	H	E	S	E	I	N	S	U	I	N	G
S	O	N	N	E	T	S	M	R	W	H	A	L	L	H	A
P	P	I	N	E	S	S	E	A	N	D	T	H	A	T	E
T	E	R	N	I	T	I	E	P	R	O	M	I	S	E	D
B	Y	O	U	R	E	V	E	R	L	I	V	I	N	G	P
O	E	T	W	I	S	H	E	T	H	T	H	E	W	E	L
L	W	I	S	H	I	N	G	A	D	V	E	N	T	U	R
E	R	I	N	S	E	T	T	I	N	G	F	O	R	T	H

It appears, therefore, that the encypherer was adept enough work with diagonals too, creating cyphers in two of the four likely grids:

24	x	6	?
18	x	8	**TO ESPIE OFT WRIOTHESLEY**...
16	x	9	**HENRY**
12	x	12	?

The ROSIE LIP cypher was also discovered in a non-perfect grid, this time of 25 columns and 6 rows. However, decreasing the number of columns by one, a perfect rectangle is obtained of 24 columns and 6 rows with the words of the message again appearing on diagonals:

```
T O T H E O N L I E B E G E T T E R O F T H E S
E I N S U I N G S O N N E T S M R W H A L L H A
P P I N E S S E A N D T H A T E T E R N I T I E
P R O M I S E D B Y O U R E V E R L I V I N G P
O E T W I S H E T H T H E W E L L W I S H I N G
A D V E N T U R E R I N S E T T I N G F O R T H
```

Almost. It can be seen that the message breaks across the right hand side of the grid and continues from the left, disrupting the cypher. However, a skilled cypher-maker could be expected to understand the connection between perfect rectangles and their adjacent grids. He would, therefore, be alive to the possibility of a diagonal message in one becoming a vertical message in the other. It is plausible then, that the author constructed this cypher by reference to both the perfect rectangle and its adjacent grid.

Crucially, if the recipient of the cypher was also familiar with transposition cyphers (perhaps even if they were not), it would be a short step from spotting a partial diagonal message in a perfect rectangle grid, to investigating the adjacent grid in the hope of rendering that message in full.

Adding to these considerations the reasons already given in Part Two for believing the ROSIE LIP cypher to be genuine, it seems justifiable to include it as appearing in the 24 by 6 perfect rectangle:

24	x	6	**LET ROSIE LIP POET APE OWN**
18	x	8	**TO ESPIE OFT WRIOTHESLEY…**
16	x	9	**HENRY**
12	x	12	?

Thus, the three transposition cyphers can be seen to occur in three of the four most suitable grids. Put another way, the encypherer seems to have made good use of all but one of the four perfect rectangle grids available to him.

I say *seems* to have, because when it came to presenting the above argument to demonstrate this point, I realised that although I had scoured all the available non-perfect rectangle grids for cyphers, and found none, I had myself overlooked something. Having given it a cursory examination, I had taken Rollett's opinion at face value that there was nothing resembling a message in the most obvious perfect rectangle of all — the 12 by 12 square.

I had always felt some unease about this, particularly since there are just four grids in which the encypherer might be expected to work. Why did he leave one out? The answer — dare I say *unsurprisingly* — was that he didn't. On closer inspection, the reason why the message had not immediately been apparent became clear.

It was in Latin.

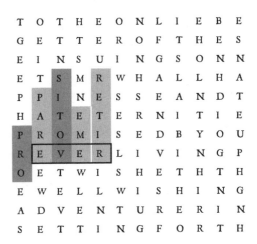

PRO... PARE... VOTIS... EMERITER...
all conjoined with that pivotal word
EVER

Quite apart from the exigencies of levering yet another gem into the already dazzlingly cypher-encrusted text of the dedication, the words comprising this last cypher are striking in their associated meanings. Taking each in turn:

PRO: Means *for* or *on behalf of* and their usual connotations in English.

PARE: Relates to the verb "pareo" with its primary sense of *"to come forth, appear, be visible, show oneself, to be present"*. A second related form is "parens" meaning *parent*, or *procreator*. There is also a third form, used by Ovid. Here the word "pare" specifically means *companion*, *mate* or *consort*.

VOTIS: Means *to vow*, *promise solemnly*, *engage religiously*, *pledge*, *devote*, *dedicate*, or *consecrate*.

EMERITER: Relates to "emeritus" meaning *to obtain by service*, *gain*, *earn*, *merit*, or *deserve*.

Playing with the order of the terms, any of the following translations might be rendered:

For my dear companion, vowing to be well-deserving, E Ver.

As here revealed, praying to earn your friendship, E Ver.

Devoutly promising to be a well-deserving father, E Ver.

The permutations of meanings are clearly numerous. What they are not is ambiguous. All the meaning clusters for the terms revolve around the relationship of desert, parentage/friendship/revelation and a promise or vow. Given that the sentence is a cypher—and one of six—some flexibility of grammatical construction might be anticipated. But most importantly, given the nature of the games the author is playing, rather than undermining the cypher, such a multiplicity of variations on a common theme is rather another example of his understanding, in this instance of Latin vocabulary, producing many meanings from just four words.

Crucially, regardless of how the translation is specified one conclusion seems unavoidable. In this last cypher to be discovered, de Vere is giving his personal signature to the dedication. In other words, *he wrote the dedication himself.* In this regard it is important to note that if the author intended the cyphers to be discovered by the recipient, the 12 by 12 grid is the *first* place one would expect a cypher-literate person to look. And the reward for their trouble would be a dedicatory message from the author himself.

The PRO PARE cypher completes the list of occupants of the four most suitable perfect rectangle grids:

24	x	6	**LET ROSIE LIP POET APE OWN**
18	x	8	**TO ESPIE OFT WRIOTHESLEY …**
16	x	9	**HENRY**
12	x	12	**PRO PARE VOTIS EMERITER EVER**

Summary of the cyphers

Before going on to examine the wider consequences of the set of hidden texts contained within the *SONNETS* dedication, it is worth summarising what has been discovered in order to appreciate the breathtaking ingenuity of the feat accomplished by the author. The range of encryption techniques employed is encyclopaedic, and includes:

An *acrostic cypher* relating the layout of the dedication to the name "Edward de Vere" (p46).

A *numerical cypher,* 6-2-4, relating the number of letters in the name "Edward de Vere" to the message "these sonnets all by ever the forth", stating that de Vere is the author of the poems (p47).

A *translation cypher* relating "the forth" to "de Vierde" a pun on the Dutch connection of the de Vere name (p52).

An *anagram cypher* relating "our ever-living poet" to "vero nil verius poet", the de Vere family motto (p56).

Four *transposition cyphers*:

HENRY, the forename of Wriothesley, one of the prime candidates as the subject/recipient of the sonnets (p60).

TO ESPIE OFT WRIOTHESLEY WIT NEED NOT HERE TRIE — a direct statement that many of the sonnets are about Wriothesley (p62).

LET ROSIE LIP POET APE OWN — a statement identifying the author of sonnet 116 (the "de Vere" sonnet) as — or as the "owner" of — the Poet-ape referred to in Sidney's *Defense of Poesie* and Jonson's *On Poet-Ape* (p64).

PRO PARE VOTIS EMERITER EVER—a Latin signature dedication within the dedication (p79).

It is not credible, I would contend, that messages of this complexity and relevance could materialise by chance in the dedication to the *SONNETS*.

Of the transposition cyphers, only the first, HENRY, might be plausibly dismissed as a coincidence. The second, TO ESPIE OFT WRIOTHESLEY WIT NEED NOT HERE TRIE, is simply too long to have fluked into existence, naming the chief candidate for the Fair Youth in the midst of the dedication. The third, LET ROSIE LIP POET APE OWN, is rendered convincing both by its length and by its startling references to sonnet 116, Jonson's *On Poet-Ape* and Sidney's *Defense of Poesie*. The fourth, PRO PARE VOTIS EMERITER EVER, a simple, punning dedication-within-a-dedication, demonstrates conclusively that de Vere was making use of every possible opportunity to advertise his skills by incorporating a first-personal signature.

While the manner of its revelation is yet again remarkable, the fact of de Vere's authorship should no longer be surprising. The dedication encryptions express such an intimate understanding of both the sonnets and their author that even without this last signature cypher, one would be hard-pressed to deny de Vere as the likely author. With it, the conclusion becomes inescapable.

III. RESOLUTION

Having established that de Vere wrote the sonnets, and that, according to de Vere himself, they are in large measure about Henry Wriothesley, it is now possible to consider the implications of the dedication cyphers on the wider questions surrounding the publication of the *SONNETS*: to whom was the dedication addressed; when was it composed; and how did Thorpe come into possession of the manuscript in 1609?

Given the nature of the messages encyphered, the natural conclusion to draw is that the dedication was written for Wriothesley. And yet, the mysterious Mr WH seems determined to obstruct this explanation. The use of the title "Mr", at least, is no longer problematic. Firstly, whoever de Vere was addressing his words to, they were *at most* his equal in terms of rank, and very likely his inferior in age by a good number of years. Terming the dedicatee "Mister" or "Master", regardless of whether it was *strictly* true at the time, would equally serve to emphasise de Vere's senior status as poet and earl, and an affectionate friendship between an older and younger man.

But in a composition of this complexity and brilliance, it seems facile to rely on a printer's error, or a well-meaning attempt by Thorpe to conceal the identity of the dedicatee, to get around the fact that the initials "WH" are simply wrong for Wriothesley. Thus the other prime contender as the recipient of the poems, William Herbert, seems determined to be part of the story. And as the ROSIE LIP cypher reveals, there are two more characters demanding their scenes too: Ben Jonson and Sir Philip Sidney.

However, it is now possible for the first time to plot a journey for the sonnets which makes sense of the relationships of all the protagonists, and which simultaneously resolves the puzzles that have surrounded their publication for the best part of four centuries.

Beginning with the orthodox account, in 1590 when Lord Burghley was looking for a suitable husband for his granddaughter Elizabeth, he fixed his attention on the highly desirable 17-year-old Henry Wriothesley. The Stratfordian suggestion is that he enlisted the help of the most talented new poet of the day—Shake-speare—to write some poems enticing Wriothesley into marriage—the "procreation" sonnets. Thus, the Stratfordian story continues, Shake-speare met the young earl, began a relationship of patronage (as evidenced by the dedication to *Venus and Adonis* in 1593) that developed into deeper friendship, even love (evinced by the dedication to *Lucrece* of 1594) and resulted in the correspondence that ultimately became the *SONNETS*.

Jumping ahead to 1597, Burghley was match-making again and this time set his sights on another eligible 17-year-old bachelor, William Herbert, for another of his granddaughters, Bridget. Again, it is suggested, he enlisted the help of Shake-speare to sell the idea to the prospective groom. Whether Shake-speare wrote new poems for Herbert, or simply repackaged some or all of the Wriothesley sonnets, is hard to know, but Stratfordian scholars such as Katherine Duncan-Jones are happy to accept the Burghley–Shake-speare explanation connecting the sonnets to both young men.

Given that it is now known that "Shake-speare" in the above story would have to be de Vere, does it still make sense? Why, it might be wondered, would Edward de Vere, 17th Earl of Oxford, Baron Sanford, Escales and Badlesmere, Viscount Bolebec, condescend to write poems to help his social—if not political—inferior, the *arriviste* Burghley marry off his granddaughters, whether to Wriothesley or Herbert? The answer is simple enough. In 1597, Burghley wrote to de Vere specifically to ask his opinion of Herbert's suitability to marry Bridget. De Vere's interest in the match is apparent from his response:

My very good lord,

I have perused these letters, which according to your Lordships desire I have returned. I do perceive how both my Lord and Lady do persever, which doth greatly content me, for Briget's sake, whom always I have wished a good husband such as your Lordship and myself may take comfort by. And as for the articles which I perceive have been moved between your Lordship and them (referring all to your Lordship's wisdom and good liking) I will freely set down mine opinion, according to your Lordship's desire.

My Lord of Pembroke [William Herbert's father] is a man sickly and therfore it is to be gathered he desireth in his lifetime to see his son bestowed to his liking. To compass which methinks his offers very honorable, his desires very reasonable. Again being a thing agreeable to your Lordship's fatherly care and love to my daughter. A thing which for the honor, friendship, and liking I have to the match—very agreable to me —so that all parties desire but the same thing. I know no reason to delay it, but according to their desires, to accomplish it with convenient speed. And I do not doubt, but your Lordship and myself shall receive great comfort thereby. For the young gentleman, as I understand, hath been well brought up, fair conditioned, and hath many good parts in him. Thus to satisfy your Lordship I have as shortly as I can set down my opinion to my Lord's desires, notwithstanding I refer theirs, and mine own which is all one with theirs, to your Lordship's wisdom. I am sorry that I have not an able body, which might have served to attend on her Majesty in the place where she is, being especially there, whither without any other occasion than to see your Lordship I would always willingly go. September VIIIth 1597

Your Lordship's most assured, *Edward Oxenford*

The young woman Burghley was so determined to wed to "Mr WH", was de Vere's daughter. In fact, both Bridget and Elizabeth, Wriothesley's intended, were the fruit of de Vere's first marriage to Burghley's daughter, Anne. In each case, Burghley had no need to buy the services of Shake-speare to entice the young gentlemen into marriage. In each case, Shake-speare—the supposed author of the inducement—was the father of the bride-to-be. In fact, there is no reason for the idea to have been Burghley's at all, it is more than likely to have originated with de Vere.

This startling "coincidence" is traditionally, and unsurprisingly, hurried past with little or no mention in Stratfordian accounts of the genesis of the *SONNETS*. That one of the prime alternative candidates as the author of the poems should have such an intimate connection with both of the prime candidates as the recipient/inspiration of those poems is not helpful to the orthodoxy. But given what is now known, there is no coincidence here, simply a natural motive for de Vere to have become involved with Wriothesley, fall in love with him and later give the sonnets he inspired, along with an ingenious dedication, to Herbert as a gift.

There is an obstacle to this neat theory, however. Taken at face value, the dedication might be a reasonably appropriate greeting, if seen as wishing Master William Herbert a happy and fruitful marriage. But given the set of messages that have been concealed within its text, it seems anything but appropriate that de Vere would include them if he was writing the dedication specifically for Herbert.

The difficulty relates to the ROSIE LIP cypher, Poet-ape, and Sir Philip Sidney. That de Vere seems to be identifying himself as the "Poet-ape" in this cypher strongly suggests that he was responding to a subject that was at the forefront of his mind while writing the dedication. Though written in the early 1580s, Sidney's *Defense of Poesie*, containing the first mention of the Poet-ape, was *published* in 1595. It would therefore have still been topical in 1597. Indeed, as has been mentioned, with its strident delineation of the rules of poetry and its condemnation of the poets of the public stage, the *Defense of Poesie* may have sparked the War of the Theatres. Furthermore, if Jonson, a key protagonist in that conflict, chose the term "Poet-ape" deliberately after Sidney, this could date *On Poet-Ape* to 1597, or even earlier.

Thus, if de Vere were writing the dedication in 1597, he would expect the recipient to understand that he was attacking Sidney and upbraiding Jonson too, via the message "let rosie lip poet ape own". Sidney, it has been noted, was regarded with something approaching reverence by the poets and courtiers of the day. And following his untimely death in 1586, the keeper of the flame of Sidney's brilliance was his beloved sister Mary, and the same Mary, Countess of Pembroke, was William Herbert's mother. If he decoded the ROSIE LIP cypher, Herbert would surely understand it as a less-than-flattering reference to his much-missed uncle.

It might be wondered if de Vere's self-identification with the Poet-ape could be taken as a merely ironic nod in the direction of Sidney. But of all those poets Sidney castigated for turning their hand to writing for the playhouses, none would have felt the sting of the Poet-ape jibe as sharply as de Vere himself. If the insult had been revived by Jonson around 1597, it would have re-opened a wound that had been festering in de Vere's heart for the best part of 20 years.

From the early 1570s until his death in 1586, Sir Philip Sidney and de Vere were to all intents and purposes mortal enemies. In 1571, Sidney was engaged to marry Anne Cecil, the daughter of Lord Burghley. The match was called off at short notice, and Burghley, denying any foreknowledge of the Earl of Oxford's interest, agreed her marriage to de Vere. As the 1570s progressed, these two highly-favoured courtiers ended up in differing factions regarding the Queen's proposed marriage to the French — and Catholic — Duke d'Alençon.

In 1579, their simmering feud reached boiling point. In a notorious incident on a tennis court, de Vere humiliated his social inferior Sidney after a furious row by pulling rank and ordering him off the court—in front of a number of French dignitaries. When Sidney, contrary to the rules of etiquette, then attempted to manoeuvre de Ver into challenging him to a duel, the Queen herself called the hot-blooded young poets to order. They were never reconciled.

In 1591, Sidney's collection of sonnets written to Lady Penelope Devereux entitled *Astrophel and Stella* was published. This first English sonnet cycle was hugely influential, cementing Sidney's status as the greatest poet of the age, and as Katherine Duncan-Jones comments, "was one of Shakespeare's most important models, and probably the sequence he most wished to 'overgo'."

In a nutshell, if "let rosie lip poet ape own" was a joke, it was a very black one. Suggesting as it does that de Vere has had the final victory over Sidney, that the author of "rosie lip" (de Vere) owns, or is the master over, the author of "poet ape" (Sidney), the sentiment hardly seems appropriate if directed towards Herbert. If the intention of the gift of the poems was to encourage Herbert to marry de Vere's daughter, including a statement that the poems were predominantly about his love for Wriothesley, and a statement that the author had triumphed in poesie over the recipient's revered uncle is counter-intuitive to say the least.

It is difficult to avoid the conclusion that de Vere did not write the dedication *for* Herbert. And yet the timing of the gift, 1597, would have been perfect, and it is Herbert's initials that appear in the dedication. Could de Vere have given the sonnets and the dedication to him anyway, even if they were written for someone else?

It is possible. Supposing de Vere had collected his poems together and crafted the ingenious dedication for another party, then the simultaneous gift of the whole to Herbert would serve a double purpose. On the one hand, de Vere would be presenting the finest of his poetic works as a mark of respect to a prospective son-in-law. On the other hand he would surreptitiously be having the last word in a contest begun more than 20 years previously with his great rival.

Without an explicit nod from de Vere that the cyphers existed, Herbert might simply take the dedication at face value. If he did unravel some or all of the hidden messages he might be offended, or he might be impressed by the wit and skill their concealment demonstrated. Either way, from de Vere's perspective, this would be a very different matter to explicitly instructing Herbert to uncover the cyphers, as he might instruct the person for whom the dedication was actually written.

Did de Vere collect the sonnets together in 1597 for another reason, then, and write the dedication in the same year for a different recipient, but gift the whole to Herbert, too? There are good reasons to suppose that this is precisely what happened, and that the primary recipient was, naturally, Henry Wriothesley.

Firstly, it was in 1597 that de Vere sold Fisher's Folly, his palatial London residence and downsized, with his wife and son, to the relatively modest seclusion of King's Place in Hackney, which was then a suburban village some distance from the Court. This retirement from political and social affairs, while not total, meant that he was rarely at Court from then until his death in 1604, and in his letters from 1597 onwards he made repeated excuses for non-attendance, due to his lameness and failing health.

Secondly, at the same moment, Henry Wriothesley's life was in turmoil. Since 1595, he had been involved in an affair with the cousin of the Earl of Essex, Elizabeth Vernon. They were apparently deeply in love, and wished to be wed with all haste. The Queen, for reasons unknown, but possibly to do with the falling from favour of Essex, was greatly displeased with the couple and refused to sanction the match. In 1597 a crisis was precipitated when Elizabeth Vernon fell pregnant. With the blessing of the Queen still unforthcoming, the lovers married without her consent. Retribution was swift, and Wriothesley and his new bride were banished from the Queen's favour—and her Court—for good.

Thus, the year 1597 marked a momentous turning point in the lives of both de Vere and Wriothesley. Under clouds of only slightly differing complexion, both left the favour of their Queen behind them, and perhaps also drew a final line under the profound relationship that had fuelled de Vere's poetic invention over the preceding seven years. If he was indeed saying farewell not only to his Queen, but also to his muse, at this moment, then the desire to bring those poems together and present them to their inspirer would have been strong.

Composing the dedication

My hypothesis, then, is that in 1597 de Vere sat down to compose a fitting dedication to his muse, to accompany this parting gift that would be a wedding gift too, on the occasion of Wriothesley's imminent marriage. At the same time, with the publication of his old adversary Sidney's great treatise, the *Defense of Poesie*, and Jonson's scathing *On Poet-Ape* ringing in his ears, he could be forgiven a strong urge to assert that the "lowly" stage poet that Sidney scorned, and perhaps the true pen shielded from Jonson's jabbing by the "Poet-ape" at the Globe, was Edward de Vere, Shake-speare himself.

Thus, there is both humour and piquancy in the messages woven into the dedication, all ready to be unpicked by anyone who knew where to look, had a quick mind, good Latin, and a smattering of Dutch. There is good reason, too, to suppose that de Vere was well-versed in the methods of cryptography. His boyhood interest could easily have been sparked by the arrival of *Steganographia* into the great library of Cecil House, where de Vere was a 13-year-old ward of Lord Burghley. As he progressed through his teens, his interest in code-makers clearly continued. At the age of 21, de Vere commissioned—and wrote a verse introduction to—the first English translation of Jerome Cardano's meditative discourse on the travails of human existence, *Cardanus' Comfort*. De Vere was certainly an admirer of the inventor of the Cardano Grille, and since the philosopher/magus was a known guest at the English Court in the late 1550s, it is possible de Vere could have later known him personally.

Sitting at his desk, de Vere would first decide the number of letters to use for the dedication. He chose 144, knowing that this perfect square delivers four good-sized perfect rectangles in which to secrete vertical cyphers. Next he drew out the grids: 12 by 12, 16 by 9, 18 by 8 and 24 by 6. Then with chalk, perhaps, or counters bearing individual letters, he began to play.

He had a good idea of the messages he wished to incorporate: something like the statement "these poems are all by Edward de Vere"; the de Vere motto as "our ever-living"; the name "Henry Wriothesley" and an indication that he is the central figure in the poems. He also planned to reveal the first of the messages with the 6-2-4 key, so knew that the positioning of the words of that message was critical.

Placing "our ever-living poet" somewhere near the centre of each of the four grids, de Vere began to weave the texts together. Trial and error, coupled with his sense of mischief and facility with language, gradually enabled him to develop the cyphers, while simultaneously watching them dissolve into the innocent message. A secretary hand "S" became a "G" and the family motto was concealed. "Henry" remained stubbornly isolated, while "Wriothesley" became the centrepiece of a beautifully elaborate sentence, and the scholarly Latin sign-off "pro pare votis emeriter ever" added another dimension of expedient erudition. Stumped for a way to end the innocent message, perhaps de Vere suddenly lit on the "forth/Vierde" pun in the dark hours of the night, mulling over a letter from his cousin Francis, bringing news of the Netherlands' conflict. Over a period of many hours, or days, or weeks—who knows how long it took—he perfected the dazzling cyphers.

The ROSIE LIP cypher, far from being idiosyncratic, was the most piquant of all. In addition to its ripostes to Sidney and Jonson, the reference to sonnet 116 could not be more emotionally charged, nor more appropriate as a resolute farewell to a lover departing to be wed, with its vow of eternal steadfastness:

116.

L et me not to the marriage of true mindes
Admit impediments, love is not love
Which alters when it alteration findes,
Or bends with the remover to remove.
O no, it is an ever fixed marke
That lookes on tempests and is never shaken;
It is the star to every wandring barke,
Whose worths unknowne, although his higth be taken.
Lov's not Times foole, though rosie lips and cheeks
Within his bending sickles compasse come,
Love alters not with his breefe houres and weekes,
But beares it out even to the edge of doome:
If this be error and upon me proved,
I never writ, nor no man ever loved.

Its singular appropriateness even provokes the suspicion that this poem was inspired by the occasion.

Finally, given that the overall message of the dedication — "To the onlie begetter…" — was not so much chosen, as arrived at as the best solution of all the encrypted texts, it is nevertheless remarkably appropriate too. The "onlie begetter" is of course — in *every* sense — Wriothesley, and the "ever-living poet" is the then-living author, de Vere, who given his state of health in 1597 would no doubt have enjoyed the morbid irony of eternalising himself as the future deceased. On its most straightforward level, the sentiment is simply: "To my inspiration, I wish you happiness and healthy children as you embark on your marriage," fitting enough for a man about to be wed, particularly if his bride-to-be was already pregnant.

Fixing the date of composition of the dedication in 1597 gives a strong motivation for de Vere to present the sonnets to Wriothesley, and the currency of the Poet-ape slur from Sidney via Jonson makes de Vere's response to it particularly apt at this time, too. Did de Vere, then, make another copy of the manuscript with the specific intention of presenting it to Herbert?

In this regard, four facts are worth bearing in mind. Firstly, on the surface level, the dedication is still appropriate as directed at Herbert, for precisely the reasons just given in regard to Wriothesley. In particular, as a mark of incipient paternalism, for de Vere to refer to the teenaged, not-yet-earl as "Master William Herbert"—Mr WH—was endearing rather than impertinent. Secondly, situated as it is in the most obvious 12 by 12 grid, the PRO PARE cypher is wholly appropriate for Herbert, too, especially if interpreted as something like:

"Devoutly promising to be a well-deserving *father*, E Ver."

In other words, as long as Herbert did not appreciate that there were *more* hidden messages, he might easily be flattered with what he did find to be concealed.

Thirdly, the idea that though Wriothesley was the primary recipient de Vere planned the wider circulation of the poems seems to be born out by Francis Meres's previously referred to remarks of 1598:

> As the soule of Euphorbus was thought to live in
> Pythagoras : so the sweet wittie soule of Ovid lives
> in mellifluous & honytongued Shakespeare, witnes
> his Venus and Adonis, his Lucrece, his sugred
> Sonnets among his private frinds, &c.

Meres indicates here that by 1598, some—or all—of Shake-speare's sonnets were in circulation, if only amongst a select group of his admirers. If de Vere presented the sonnets as a personal and very private gift to Wriothesley in late 1597, it seems less rather than more likely that the poems would have been in circulation as soon as 1598. As a private gift from an ex-lover, Wriothesley might have wanted to keep the poems to himself. Given also that he was barred from the Court before 1598 had even begun, he would have been perhaps excluded from the company of precisely those "private frinds" to whom Meres refers, and hence unable to share the poems with them.

Thus it could well be that while the gift was undoubtedly primarily for Wriothesley, de Vere gave copies of the edition to others, particularly if his motivation was to formally mark that Shake-speare the sonneteer was laying down his pen.

Fourthly, there is a final peculiarity of the dedication that is relevant here. Below, the text is presented with every letter that has been used in a cypher marked in grey:

TO.THE.ONLIE.BEGETTER.OF.
THESE.INSVING.SONNETS.
MR.W.H. ALL.HAPPINESSE.
AND.THAT.ETERNITIE.
PROMISED.
BY.

OVR.EVER-LIVING.POET.
WISHETH.

THE.WELL-WISHING.
ADVENTVRER. IN
SETTING.
FORTH.

It can be seen that neither of the initials "WH" are cypher letters. This implies that *any* initials can be used in the dedication without disturbing the hidden messages. I believe, therefore, that while composing the dedication de Vere deliberately ensured that changing the initials would not destroy any of the cyphers, allowing him to re-use the same dedication for a number of different recipients.

It would make pragmatic sense, at least, if William Herbert was one of those other recipients. By 1597, de Vere was effectively isolated from the Court, he no longer even owned the roof over his own head, and with his health failing, the ambition to see his daughter tie the bloodlines of the earldoms of Oxford and Pembroke would surely have been at the forefront of his mind, regardless of his personal history with Sidney.

In his heyday, as well as being a poet himself, de Vere had been one of the most influential poet patrons, both in directly supporting writers in diverse disciplines and through his theatrical companies. But in 1597 his star was dimmed, and the next generation of patrons — led by Wriothesley, with Herbert and others hot on his heels — was about to eclipse him altogether. Embodying de Vere's prowess and legacy in the area of human endeavour that mattered most of all to Herbert — poetry — the sonnets would have made a perfect gift for the young earl-to-be in his 17th year. On the surface, an entreaty to unite two of the most eminent aristocratic and literary dynasties, but secretly allowing de Vere to serve the winning ace in a duel begun on a tennis court 30 years before.

• • •

Thus, there is a consistent explanation for all the facts so far. In 1590, de Vere became acquainted with the 17-year-old Wriothesley, and wrote 17 sonnets for him with a view to encouraging a match with his daughter Elizabeth. As their relationship developed, de Vere wrote first *Venus and Adonis* in 1593, and then *Lucrece* in 1594, as well as continuing a steady output of sonnets diarising his intimate relationship with his young friend. In 1597, de Vere collected the sonnets together (commencing with the 17 "procreation" sonnets, the first he had written to Wriothesley) as a poignant farewell both to sonneteering and to his lover, wrote the dedication to him, and presented the whole as a gift for Wriothesley's wedding, addressed to "Mr HW". Changing the initials, de Vere also presented a copy to the 17-year-old Herbert as a token of esteem in a bid to flatter him into marrying his daughter Bridget. By 1598, Herbert's copy was in circulation, though others may have been too. In 1599, two of the sonnets were published by William Jaggard in *The Passionate Pilgrim*, prompting a staying order in the Stationers' Register in 1600.

Overall, it is a scenario that would be plausible even without the discovery of the dedication cyphers. With those covert messages added to the picture, it becomes compelling.

EPILOGUE

O f the many puzzles with which this book began, only two remain to be unravelled. Firstly, why did this personal gift to Herbert come to be in the hands of Thomas Thorpe in 1609? Secondly, why did the book he then published, *SHAKE-SPEARES SONNETS*, disappear, seemingly without trace, almost immediately after its publication?

It is clear from what has gone before that in 1609 or thereabouts, Thomas Thorpe received the manuscript of the sonnets complete with the dedication, and that he affixed his initials to it, knowing it was not his own work. It has also been argued that Thorpe's edition was not a work of piracy. In other words, he received the manuscript, if not from the author himself, then at least from an authorised source. Thirdly, by 1609, Thorpe was a skilled and reputable publisher; if he had wanted to present the poems in a more marketable way, with the grandstanding dedication and commendatory verses that might be considered fitting for the author of *Venus and Adonis*, he was perfectly capable of doing so.

It seems reasonable to conclude that in publishing the *SONNETS* in the low-key but professional way he did, Thorpe was sticking to a format that was dictated by the person who had provided the manuscript to him—including the instruction to put his own initials to the dedication. Given what has been demonstrated regarding the true nature of that dedication, the explanation for this inclusion is quite simple. Thorpe's initials would encourage a reader to accept the dedication at face value, and not enquire any further into its meaning, whereas the absence of initials might provoke curiosity.

This implies that whoever requested Thorpe to publish the sonnets also wanted the dedication to appear as it was originally written, including the name "Mr WH". There is one candidate with perfect motive, opportunity, and timing for such a move: William Herbert.

In the plague-blighted spring of 1609, the machinery of government was working overtime to promote one of the greatest projects England had ever known, one that it hoped would unite the realm in an outpouring of nationalistic optimism. Three years previously, a Royal Charter had created a joint stock enterprise, the London Company, with the express aim of establishing viable English colonies in North America as part of the continuing struggle to gain control of the territory and resources of the New World. The venture had so far met with mixed success. The establishment of a first settlement at Jamestown was faltering, hampered by illness, attacks from the understandably annoyed indigenous population and disputes between the members of the Crown-appointed council and the settlers.

By 1609, the entire project was in a make or break position. The potential rewards of success were enormous, but the problems of governance were making investors jittery. A huge media campaign began in London to re-invigorate the enterprise and encourage the country as a whole to dig into its pockets to back it. The printing presses churned out broadsides announcing the rich pickings awaiting those willing to set forth across the atlantic, or at least to finance those brave enough to go. From pulpits across England, clergymen pronounced that—for his part—God was certainly fully supportive of such colonial aspirations.

As anticipation mounted, the original backers of the newly christened "Virginia Company" renegotiated terms allowing investors greater control over subsequent colonies, and the Second Charter of Virginia was drawn up. Listed in order of precedence were over 650 "adventurers" as they were referred to in the Charter, each of whom had paid at least the minimum £12 10s stake. After the mighty earls of Salisbury and Suffolk, third and fourth on that list came the earls of Southampton and Pembroke, Henry Wriothesley and William Herbert.

On 15 May 1609, preparations had been made, and a great fleet of nine vessels, lead by Sir George Summers aboard the *Sea Adventure*, set off down the Thames to Plymouth, from whence they would set sail for the New World on 2 June. The Charter itself would be brought into effect by King James on 23 May.

It is not difficult to imagine the Earl of Pembroke, now in the ascendency in the Court of King James, being keen to demonstrate his standing among his co-investors. Indeed, his commitment to the enterprise was such that by 1618 he would become the principal stakeholder in the Virginia Company. And in the gift made to him by a prospective father-in-law 12 years previously, he would have enjoyed a coincidence of language in the dedication that was a perfect—if slightly convoluted—fit for the occasion, if read as:

> *"To the recipient of the following sonnets: Mr WH wishes*
> *the adventurer all happiness and fruitful returns as*
> *promised by the author."*

Herbert's intention would have been that investors in the project have a souvenir from the Earl of Pembroke himself to mark the great occasion of the signing of the Charter. Yes, perhaps it is necessary to crowbar the meaning into compliance—but from the point of view of Herbert's purpose, for once that is *not* a major issue. That this most malleable of texts should be pressed into service one last time, its richly ambiguous phrasing serving up yet another layer of meaning, is a fitting finale to the story. And being largely intended for his peers, Herbert would be happy to refer to himself—in all humility of course—as "Mr WH".

Why though, did Herbert choose Thorpe for the task of publishing? I believe he did not. Rather, he entrusted the project to the chief talent among his poet clique, the writer to whom he would send £20 each New Year's Day to furnish his library: Ben Jonson. It would be little surprise if Jonson then took the manuscript straight to his most trusted publisher, and perhaps still at that point friend, Thomas Thorpe, with instructions to lay the poems out strictly according to the manuscript, to insert his own initials after the dedication, and to have the copies of the *SONNETS*—enough to occupy two booksellers—ready before 23 May.

And when the day of the signing of the Second Virginia Charter arrived, were all the copies snapped up by the excited investors? Or did Herbert commandeer some or all of the copies, perhaps to bestow as personal gifts without reimbursing Thorpe? There is no way of knowing as yet, though, according to Duncan-Jones, in 1609 Herbert was out-spending his means, so it is a possibility that Thorpe was short-changed. However things turned out, it the episode might have been enough to sour relations between Thorpe and Jonson. If the latter's remarks in the dedication to Herbert of his own collected epigrams (page 35) were indeed directed at the *SONNETS* dedication, he viewed that publication with a lofty condescension bordering on animosity. How much Jonson knew about the provenance of the *SONNETS*—and Shake-speare—is an intriguing question for another day. But at the least, it seems the affair placed too great a strain on his relationship with his favoured publisher. They never collaborated again.

And despite being the nominal holder of the copyright, Thorpe never republished the *SONNETS*. But why would he? Even if the first edition had been well received, he would not risk angering the true "owner" by publishing again without Herbert's express permission. And if publishing the *SONNETS* was Herbert's vanity project, an exercise in self-publicity, there would be little reason for him to repeat it. Life, after all, moves on. And thus the final mystery dissolves, for it is no longer any surprise that it would not be until after the death of both Herbert and Thorpe that John Benson would bring de Vere's poems to the attention of the world once again.

• • •

In the case of the authorship of the Shake-speare canon, perhaps a tipping point has now been reached. In the same way that the Jovian satellites and the phases of Venus were the final straw that caused the earth-centred cosmology to collapse, the cyphers described in this book are quite straightforwardly *facts*, which render the Stratfordian paradigm untenable. Of course, just as Copernicus's new theory was elaborated in the wake of Galileo's discoveries, the way is now open for more detailed investigation of circumstances only sketched herein.

Principle among these questions is of course *why* de Vere published under a pseudonym at all. In the case of the *SONNETS*, I have suggested that the concealment is in no small measure a *conceit*, part of an elaborate game indulged in by a generation of new writers intoxicated by the possibilities of the written word. It is also likely that the sensitive nature of the content and the high rank of the subject of the poems necessitated a degree of circumspection, a line of defence at least against the reputation-destroying accusation of pederasty, which was then still a capital, if rarely prosecuted, offence. Why *William Shake-speare* was the name adopted, and whether de Vere was alone in publishing under it is, in the wider context of the plays of the *First Folio,* a fascinating area for investigation. That research is already well under way, and my hope is that this book will convince scholars from both sides of the Authorship divide to pool their resources to explore it fully.

We have come a long way from the initial suggestion that the 30 words prefacing the first edition of the most famous poems in the English language are the awkward solicitations of an inept and piratical publisher. The dedication has now been revealed as what it truly is—a work of art in itself. Combining multi-faceted encryptions within its innocent-seeming text, it is a brilliantly executed cryptological fugue, showcasing a supreme ability in illusion, allusion, concealing and *revealing* meanings. Not the least of which being that the author of *SHAKE-SPEARES SONNETS*, and the enigmatic dedication itself, was Edward de Vere.

FINIS

REFERENCES

Author's note: In all areas of discussion except where referring to the specific arguments of anti-Stratfordian scholars, references cited in support of the arguments presented in this book come only from Stratfordian, or neutral, sources.

p.i. *Shake-speares Sonnets* title page, reproduced from *Shakespeares Sonnets*, Sidney Lee (ed), 1895, p79.

p.ii. *Shake-speares Sonnets* dedication, *ibid.* p81.

p. xiii. Galileo Galilei, *Dialogue on the Great World Systems* (1632), Thomas Salusbury translation (1661), ed. Giorgio de Santillana, Cambridge Univ. Press, London; 1953.

p. xv. History of the telescope… Fred Watson, *Stargazer: the life and times of the telescope*, Da Capo Press; chapter 3.

p. xvi. Galileo Galilei, *The Sidereal Messenger* (1610) translated by Edward Stafford Clark, Dawsons, London 1880; p44-45.

p. xvii. Galileo's code… David Kahn, *The Codebreakers*, Scribner, 1996; p773.

p. xix. Index of Prohibited Books… *ibid.* p132.

p. xix. Ovid… *ibid.* p774.

p. xx. "perform the very disappearing act…" Jonathan Bate, *The Genius of Shakespeare*, Picador, 1997; p64.

p. xx. "penning exercises in style…" *ibid.* p42.

p. xxii. John Michel, *Who Wrote Shakespeare?*, Thames & Hudson, 1997.

p. xxiv. Ben Jonson, *Timber, or Discoveries Made Upon Men and Matter*, 1640.

p.3. "killing up to a hundred…" Katherine Duncan-Jones (ed), *Shakespeare's Sonnets*, The Arden Shakespeare, 1997; p11.

p.5. "Suppression was ruthless…" Bryan Thomas Herek, *Early Modern Satire and the Bishop's Order of 1599: Manuscript, Print and Stage*, (PhD thesis), http://www.lib.umd.edu/drum/bitstream/1903/2696/1/umi-umd-2624.pdf.

p.5. "issue of copyright…" Lyman Ray Patterson, *Copyright in historical perspective*, Vanderbilt University Press, 1968; p29 ff.

p.7. Reception of the sonnets… Duncan-Jones, p70.

p.8. Francis Meres, *ibid.* p1.

p.8. "in important respects…", *ibid.* p46.

p.9. Surviving copies… Andrew Murphy, *Shakespeare in Print*, Cambridge University Press, 2003; p18

p.9. "a certain covetousness…" James Schiffer, *Reading New Life into Shakespeare's Sonnets: A survey of Criticism*, reprinted in *Shakespeare's Sonnets: Critical Essays, Routledge*, 2000; p58.

p.10. Thorpe's retirement… Sidney

Lee, *A Life of William Shakespeare*,1899, Smith, Elder and Co; p279.

p.11. "underhand" Stanley Wells, *Shakespeare for all time*, Oxford University Press, 2003; p177.

p.11. "unforgivable injuries" John Kerrigan, *Shakespeare's Sonnets*, Penguin Classics, 1999.

p.11. "outrageously piratical" Duncan-Jones, p42.

p.15. "basis for every reprinting" Richard Dutton, Jean Elizabeth Howard, *A Companion to Shakespeare's Works: Poems, problem comedies, late plays*, Blackwell, 2003; p15.

p.16. Thorpe biography…Veronica Palmer, *Who's Who in Shakespeare's England*, St Martin's Press, 1981; p250.

p.16. "division of labour…" Lyman Ray Patterson, *Copyright in historical perspective*, Vanderbilt University Press, 1968; p46.

p.17. Dedication to Blount… Christopher Marlowe, *Complete Works*, AH Bullen (ed), JC Nimmo, 1885; p249.

p.18. Jonson and *Isle of Dogs*… Rosalind Miles, *Ben Jonson: His Life and Work*, Routlege & Keegan Paul, 1986; p31.

p.18. Jonson kills Spencer… *ibid*, p33.

p.18. Jonson beats Marston… Phillip Sidney (ed), *Conversations of Ben Jonson with William Drummond*, Gay & Bird, 1906; p22.

p.19. Poet-ape is Shaksper…

Marilyn Randall, *Pragmatic plagiarism: authorship, profit, and power*, University of Toronto Press, 2001; p104.

p.19. David Mann, *The Elizabethan player: contemporary stage representation*, Routledge, 1991 p101.

p.19. Description of Jonson… Sidney, p62.

p.20. William Fennor on Jonson… Marchette Chute, *Ben Jonson of Westminster*, EP Dutton & Co, 1953; p116.

p.20. *Sejanus* preface… Project Gutenberg *EBook of Sejanus: His Fall, by Ben Jonson*, EBook #5232, www.gutenberg.org/ files/5232/5232.txt.

p.22. "The exactness of…" Jonas Barish (ed), *Ben Jonson, Sejanus: His Fall*, Yale, 1965; p205.

p.22. "well born or scholarly…" Miles, p99.

p.23. "The only other sonnet sequence to do likewise…" Duncan-Jones, p85.

p.25. Bertrand Russell, *Autobiography*, Routledge, 2000, p601.

p.25. "one of the elaborate…" Bate, p62.

p.27. William Hall as Mr WH… Sidney Lee, p92.

p.29. "the case for Southampton…" Bate, p49.

p.30. "slandering a prince" Miles, p94.

p.31. "every New Year's Day" Sidney, p35.

p.31. Herbert's affair… Margaret

P. Hanna, *Philip's phoenix: Mary Sidney, Countess of Pembroke*; p169.

p.31. "overwhelmingly attractive" Duncan-Jones, p69.

p.32. "A book called Amours…" *ibid.* p3.

p.32. "The Herbert case…" *ibid.* p69.

p.33. *City of God…* Lee, p289.

p.33. "ever-living" Bate, p63.

p.34. Addenbrooke debt… Samuel Schoenbaum, *William Shakespeare: a compact documentary life*, Oxford University Press, 1987; p241.

p.34. "some already dead poet…" Bate, p63.

p.34. "Supreme Poet…" Donald W Foster. *Master W. H., R.I.P*, PMLA (1987), 42-54.

p.41. "Sometimes it is suspected…" Bate, p65.

p.42. "On the balance of evidence…" John Michel, *Who Wrote Shakespeare?*, Thames & Hudson, 1997.

p.44. "In this common shipwreck…" Alan H Nelson, "Personal Letter no.39", *Letters and Memoranda of Edward de Vere 17th earl of Oxford*, available at http://socrates.berkeley.edu/~ahnelson/oxlets.html

p.46. John M Rollett, *Secrets of the Dedication to Shakespeare's Sonnets*, Oxfordian 2 (1999): 60-75.

p.46. Dedication as Roman inscription… Duncan-Jones, p60.

p.47. Antony Munday acrostic…

Tracey Hill, *Anthony Munday and civic culture*, Manchester University Press 2004, p84.

p.47. "Jonson was fond of them too" Miles, p48.

p.48. "Ann Vavasour's Echo" Robert Brazil & Barboura Flues, *Poems of Edward de Vere, 17th Earl of Oxford*, no.16, www.elizabethanauthors.com/oxfordpoems.htm.

p.49. John M Rollett, *Shakespeare Fellowship Forums*, www.shakespearefellowship.org/ubbthreads/ubbthreads.php/ubb/showthreaded/Number/15642/site_id/1#import.

p.50. GE Cokayne, *The Complete Peerage of England, Scotland, Ireland, Great Britain and the United Kingdom* (1895), Volume 6, George Bell & Sons; p161.

p.51. "Having no other means…" Nelson, "Personal Letter no.2".

p.51. Dutch war of independence… Clements R Markham, *The Fighting Veres* (1888), Sampson Low, Marston, Searle & Rivington Ltd; piii.

p.51. "If there were any service…" Nelson, "Personal Letter no.4".

p.52. "In that fight there were…" Markham, p1.

p.53. Sir Henry Neville… Brenda James and William D Rubenstein, *The Truth Will Out: Unmasking the Real Shakespeare*, Pearson, 2006.

p.56. Michel, p181.

p.56. *The Principal, Historical, and Allusive Arms, Borne by Families of the United Kingdom of Great*

Britain and Ireland, with Their Respective Authorities (1803), J Nichols & Son; p449.

p.57. *A Newe Book of Copies*, Vautrollier, 1574.

p57. Anagrams… RH Winnick, *"Loe, here in one line is his name twice writ": Anagrams, Shakespeare's Sonnets, and the Identity of the Fair Friend*, in *Literary Imagination*, OUP (online edition), 4 October 2009.

p.59. "An astrologer by trade…" Anthony Grafton, *Cardano's cosmos: the worlds and works of a Renaissance astrologer*, Harvard University Press, 2001; p112.

p.66. "the cause why it is not esteemed…" Henry Morley (ed), *Sir Philip Sidney, A Defence of Poesy and Poems*, 1891, Cassell & Co; p97.

p.66. "but I have lavished…" *ibid.* p89.

p.69. "It is also worth noting…" Paul Alpers, *Learning from the New Criticism: The Example of Shakespeare's Sonnets*, in Renaissance Literature and its formal Engagements, Mark D Rasmussen (ed), Palgrave, 2002; p126.

p.69. "sets up an ideal of true love…" Duncan-Jones, p342.

p.69. Heraldic badge… Terence Wise, Richard Hook, William

Walker, *Medieval heraldry*, 1980, Osprey; p19.

p.70. "the night coming on…" John Leland, *Itinerary*, vol 6, pp37-8, 1744 ed, in *The Origin of Tragedy*, William Ridgeway, p84.

p.80. PRO, PARE, VOTIS, EMERITER… Charlton T. Lewis, Charles Short, *A Latin Dictionary*, Perseus Digital Library Project. Ed. Gregory R. Crane. Tufts University, www.perseus.tufts.edu.

p.80. Ovid's use of PARE… Frederick Percival Leverett, *A New and copious lexicon of the Latin language*, 1837, Wilkins & Carter; p620.

p.89. "My very good lord…" Nelson, "Personal Letter no.29".

p.91. Sidney and de Vere… Sir Fulke Greville, *Life of Sir Philip Sidney: Etc.*, 1652; p63.

p.92. "most wished to "overgo'"… Duncan-Jones, p85.

p.97. Meres… Duncan-Jones, p1.

p.104. Second Virginia Charter… Wesley Frank Craven, *The Virginia Company Of London*, 1606-1624, April 11, 2009 [EBook #28555].

p.105. "principal stakeholder…" Duncan-Jones, p58.

p.106. "spending beyond his means…" *ibid.* p58.

INDEX

If you would like to comment on THE DE VERE CODE, or find out more about Edward de Vere and the works of SHAKE-SPEARE, or order more copies of the book, please visit:

www.deverecode.com